The Nature of Marketing

Marketing to the Swarm as well as the Herd

Chuck Brymer

palgrave
macmillan

First published 2009 by
PALGRAVE MACMILLAN

Palgrave Macmillan in the UK is an imprint of Macmillan Publishers Limited,
registered in England, company number 785998, of Houndmills, Basingstoke,
Hampshire RG21 6XS.

Palgrave Macmillan in the US is a division of St Martin's Press LLC,
175 Fifth Avenue, New York, NY 10010.

Palgrave Macmillan is the global academic imprint of the above companies
and has companies and representatives throughout the world.

Palgrave® and Macmillan® are registered trademarks in the United States,
the United Kingdom, Europe and other countries.

ISBN-13: 978-0–230–20336–5
ISBN-10: 0–230–20336–1

This book is printed on paper suitable for recycling and made from fully
managed and sustained forest sources. Logging, pulping and manufacturing
processes are expected to conform to the environmental regulations of the
country of origin.

A catalogue record for this book is available from the British Library.

A catalog record for this book is available from the Library of Congress.

10 9 8 7 6 5 4 3 2 1
18 17 16 15 14 13 12 11 10 09

Printed in China

Contents

Acknowledgements

Writing a book is either a labor of love or just plain labor, I am not sure. In my case, I wanted to write this book to reflect upon the profound influence that digital communities are having in transforming our businesses and society. Equally important, I wanted to give my take on what those of us in the marketing community need to do to capitalize on this opportunity.

There have been many people who have contributed to this effort – way too many to mention. Even my dog has gotten in the act, eating part of the original manuscript. Perhaps he didn't like what he was reading.

I do, however, want to send a call out to a few people who helped bring this to life. One of those is Jeff Swystun, a colleague of mine at DDB, who in his own diplomatic way prodded me to keep going. Another has been my assistant Ann Wrynn, who graciously reminded me that Jeff was prodding me to keep going. Lastly, of course, is my family who put up with seeing me less than they already do … something I am not sure was really a burden.

More than anyone, this book belongs to the more than 13,000 people of DDB. A global communications firm that is leading a charge into the ever-changing world of social media and swarm marketing … and whose collective curiosity is insatiable. Thank you.

Preface

I enjoy looking at predictions of the future. When I grew up in the 60s and 70s, people imagined having things like flying cars, two-way videophones worn on the wrist, and jet packs strapped to a person's back.

Today I find it interesting to hear all the people who have predicted the death of advertising, in an era of fragmented channels and online social networks.

Of course, I am biased. As the CEO of DDB Worldwide, one of the world's largest advertising agencies, you might expect me to see a bright future for advertising. But it also gives me a front-row seat to watch the dialogue between brands and their consumers, and see how this dialogue is changing over time.

Here is what I see today. Our industry has always been focused on marketing to millions of individuals sitting in front of their televisions watching our message, or surfing the Web and seeing our banner ads. If we are good at what we do, a certain percentage of these people will respond. If we are better, more of them will respond. But it has traditionally been a one-way monologue from us to them.

Now here is what I visualize for tomorrow. We will be marketing to digitally linked communities that behave as a single organism and respond quickly to points of influence. These communities are fueled by the connectivity of the Web 2.0 generation, but follow principles of behavior that researchers have seen since the dawn of time in social groups ranging from swarms of bees to early human civilizations – principles that are fundamentally changing the way we view and practice marketing.

This past decade has seen the rise of viral marketing, where people spread your brand message contagiously from person to person. More recently in the digital age, we have started talking about things like influencer marketing, where targeting the right key people or the right blogger can spread the word about your brand. And today marketing coexists in a world of alternative media channels and social networks.

Which brings me to the core concept of this book: *Digital connectivity is creating consumers who behave less like individuals, and more like a community.* Yesterday's consumers responded to advertising within the isolation of their own magazine or television set. Today's consumer posts to virtual forums, reads online ratings from other community members, and shares viral videos. Tomorrow's consumer will be even more connected. And the result is a global community that behaves the same way our ancestors did when they gathered around a bonfire; they are influenced at a community level.

Once you understand the dynamics of *any* community, real or virtual, you start to see the common thread between all of these trends. Biologists and social scientists have seen them for decades. In a community, a small number of people – sometimes even *one* person – can quickly become the voice of a hundred, a thousand, or 200 million, in much the same way that a single darting fish can move the entire school toward food or away from a predator. Think about how social movements start, or how gossip spreads, and you will understand the future of marketing better.

The key here is that these communities transcend both technology and trends. For example, look at what happens when a hot new viral video spreads through the blogosphere. Unlike viral marketing, the people who watch it may never speak to each other. And they are not necessarily "influencers," but rather everyday people. But their individual actions, as they flock toward their normal gathering places in a digital community, lead to a group outcome.

Communities are composed of agents who follow simple rules, which lead to a collective intelligence. So when someone posts a comment on an online rating site, or a popular band releases its new CD online, it sets off a sudden – but at the same time predictable – chain reaction across the entire social network. These new digital communities are about the power of one person, and at the same time the power of many.

What will this new, digitally connected metaverse mean for you, your brand, and your customers' reaction?

First, it will give you tremendous leverage. Later in this book, you will see how we took a tiny marketing budget and an edgy viral video and launched a category-killer personal care product. How we sold three million lightbulbs, by being where people flocked with a message that attracted them. And how we resurrected a classic board game by making a major world city its playing field.

Second, it will change the way you do business. Engaging a community goes far beyond advertising products. They will become part of your organization, and you will become part of their lives. Whether it is as direct as the toy company whose customers design their next product kits, or as virtual as the party we hosted for one client in the digital world of Second Life, we are moving from product marketing to true brand communities.

xi

Third, and perhaps most important, it will remove the very high wall that too often exists between your marketing and your brand image. Decades ago, companies could create marketing images of smiling, happy customers, while in the real world word traveled slowly about their poor products or services. Today you are one blog post away from having consumers flee from you in unison, and your humblest customer is now as powerful as your entire marketing department. But if you build a strong brand – and, more important, a strong brand community – people will flock toward you and even forgive your mistakes.

All of these things spring from a digital social movement that is fresh and new, yet truly takes us back to our roots. According to some researchers, today's social networks have a lot in common with the Chinese social customs of Guanxi from thousands of years ago, as well as the much longer history of the animal kingdom. There is now much more in common between your MySpace page and the old village square than most of us realize.[1]

This trend is also a logical extension of our own history at DDB. Even in our early days in the 1950s, we talked about creating dialogue with our customers, and our late cofounder Bill Bernbach used to say that "finding out what to say is the beginning of the communication process." Today, our own globally linked enterprise has its roots in the multidisciplinary creative teams we pioneered generations ago. So functioning in a linked social community is not just a great marketing technique, but also an extension of something that has long been a way of life for us.

This idea has now taken a life of its own. Today people are talking about communities throughout the advertising industry blogosphere, and a recent Forrester Research report now predicts an era of connected agencies that evolve from "orchestrating campaigns to facilitating conversations."[2] More important, the emergent creative behavior of this entire industry shows that we have already started moving toward engaging people at a community level, long before we started calling it that.

The dialogue we are having now is reminiscent of my earlier work in promoting and measuring the concept of brand value: It was something

1 Hammond, Scott C. and Glenn, Lowell M., "The ancient practice of Chinese social networking: Guanxi and social network theory," E:CO Special Double Issue, Vol. 6, No. 1–2, 2004, pp. 24–31.
2 Kemp, Mary Beth and Kim, Peter, "The Connected Agency," Forrester Research report, Feb. 8, 2008.

few people thought about many years ago, but is now central to the corporate balance sheet. In much the same way, I feel that engaging communities is destined to become one of the basic foundational concepts for the future of brands and marketing.

This book will show you how today's digital connectivity is kicking our natural evolutionary trends into overdrive, and examine how this will affect you and your brand. First, we look at the nature of digital communities and its roots in both animal behavior and social networking. Next, we look at how these emerging communities are changing marketing as we know it: how we are entering an age of reference, not deference, and how speed is becoming the new "big."

From there we will get to the heart of how you put these ideas to work. We explore what I feel are the three core competencies of engaging communities – conviction, collaboration, and creativity – as well as how you create the "nectar" that gets them to flock toward you. Finally, we look at how these trends will change your organization from one that sells products and services to one that truly engages your brand community, in a framework of dialogue and co-creation.

Advertising is far from dead. In fact, the kind of advertising we did half a century ago is still alive, well, and flourishing. And the energy and innovation of this field in recent years have been very exciting, as we branch out further online and deeper into the minds of our customers. But we now are entering an era that is changing the foundations of marketing – one that is fueled by technology, yet literally and figuratively based on how people have behaved for centuries.

Chuck Brymer
October 2008

CHAPTER 1

The Power of One and the Power of Many

What makes people suddenly start flocking to Canada in the middle of winter?

In early 2007, the world became transfixed by the story of Knut, a polar bear cub who was rejected by its mother after being born in captivity at the Berlin Zoo. As he survived and grew under the care of humans, he became an international celebrity, spawning books, record crowds of visitors, and even an animated movie deal.

One of these visitors was the head of the Canadian Tourism Commission (CTC) in Germany, who presented Knut with a bright red ball with its logo. Pictures of the cub playing with it were beamed around the world in major media outlets, and then these cute images spread throughout the blogosphere. Soon afterward, the Berlin Zoo and CTC hosted a contest to send one lucky winner to Manitoba to see polar bears in their natural habitat.

The result? A bright red ball and a cute cub led very quickly to a 20 percent increase in polar bear tourism to Canada. People from Germany, Japan, and elsewhere in the world suddenly started flocking to one of the coldest places on Earth for their vacation.

This type of marketing – employing people as the viral connectors to their digital communities – is having a profound impact on how we look at marketing.

Knut the polar bear cub plays with a present from the Canadian Tourism Commission at the Berlin Zoo.

Fueled by the power of social networks and media, humans are re-establishing themselves as the ultimate communicators, spreading the word across the globe at unprecedented speed. In the process, we have moved closer to the predictable behavior of other systems in nature including animal swarms.

These new human swarms represent an evolutionary next step in marketing behavior; we are progressing from a herd of individual consumers to a living, breathing organism that acts as one. It takes many of the trends of the past few years like viral marketing, social networks, and influencers, and puts them in their proper context as a broader force of nature.

A flock of birds, for example, does not practice viral marketing because no bird talks to another. Fans at a crowded sports stadium doing the "wave" are not practicing influencer marketing because there is no leader. Any one fan can set the entire crowd in motion. But they are tightly linked social networks that respond to the power of one. Now, so are we.

The birth of the global digital community

Communities are very predictable at a social level. We can even simulate much of their behavior mathematically. They are composed of independent human beings, yet react to what happens in their environment – and, more important, each other – as a source of collective intelligence.

For example, picture a group of 1200 or so volunteers. Most of them do not know or talk to each other. No one pays them or tells them what to do. But they too follow simple rules, without a leader, and in the process create much of the content of Wikipedia, the online encyclopedia that has become one of the ten most visited sites on the Internet. These volunteer editors oversee a stream of over 200,000 edits per day to a resource that can tell you anything from real-time current events to who sang lead for an obscure 1960s rock group. They are part of a community that is as real as any social group that ever existed, even though they have never met.

Now, think about what happened the last time you purchased something. Did the message of an advertiser drive that decision? Or, did the voice of an online community such as consumer ratings on Amazon.com or blogs hold more sway? Did a social network such as MySpace combine with influential peers to influence what your teenage daughter listens to or what your son in college wears? More important, did your own experiences become part of the dialogue itself? If so, you are now behaving predictably as part of a larger community. In the process, you have joined one of the biggest sociological transformations of the past century.

This is not a technological revolution, but rather a social one. Technology is a commodity now. Once upon a time, things like lightbulbs and telephones were competitive advantages, and today they aren't. The same will be true about things like social networking, blogs, and the Internet.

What is truly revolutionary is that we now think differently.

This social movement, not even a decade old, has dramatically changed the way we do business. We now live in a world where what people say about you on YouTube or Amazon.com can influence an entire population perhaps more than any agency now can, and an amazingly consistent "groupthink" about brands and products can form – or change – in a flash. This change is driven by forces that link the voices of businessmen in Bangladesh, farmers in Iowa, and homemakers in Seoul with the dialogue between people and the brands they use.

Here at DDB, we have a view of how human beings are becoming more and more connected, particularly when it comes to their brand awareness and purchasing behavior. If you are not in the advertising business, you may not recognize our name. But most of you are aware of our handiwork. When McDonald's says "I'm lovin' it," a young man drinking Bud Light yells "Whassup!" into the phone, or State Farm talks about being "like a good neighbor," you know us.

Now, here is what we know. The relationship between people and brands has undergone a fundamental shift as we have entered the second millennium. It is enabled by digital technology and a global community. But it perhaps can best be explained in the same terms as a swarm of bees or teenagers at a high school dance.

In the past, we generally used "herd" marketing techniques. We used the mass media to approach people as they sat in front of their television sets – or surfed the Internet – and pushed messages at them, hoping that a certain percentage of them would buy what we were selling. Or, more importantly, we hoped to create a brand identity that would lead enough herd members to remember us for all of their buying decisions, long after they saw our last advertisement. It was a one-to-many monologue between a product and its consumers, and we measured its success in terms of variables such as brand awareness and market penetration.

Today, we are marketing to a swarm that shares information within itself, moves in an instant, and takes direction from no one. Its members are connected to you and each other as a single living, breathing organism with digital information running through its veins. As people follow the rhythm of these social networks, we are slowly but steadily losing some of our influence on them as individuals, because we are competing with what the swarm itself tells them. At the same time, the power and potential to influence people as entire communities is making a dramatic change in the way we do marketing.

Saving the Earth – and selling three million light bulbs

On July 7, 2007, the Live Earth benefit concert event took place in cities around the world, with top musical acts performing on every continent to draw attention to the problems of global climate change.

At the same time, Live Earth was much more than a live concert event: It also became an instant community on the Internet, where nearly 15 million people watched live streams of the performances while simultaneously being challenged to look at their own personal contributions to the Earth's climate. By the end of the event, nearly half a million of them had made commitments online to make specific changes in their own personal lives to reduce the production of greenhouse gases.

Many of these commitments came from a challenge posted on the Live Earth website by sponsor Royal Philips Electronics of the Netherlands, linking people to a screen calculating the CO_2 and energy savings impact of changing to Philips compact fluorescent lightbulbs – and then

5

expanding that to what would happen if ten of their friends joined in, and urging them to invite these friends online. The net result was commitments to purchase over three million lightbulbs, with a net savings of close to a billion kilograms of carbon dioxide.

Today Philips' "A Simple Switch" website (www. asimpleswitch.com/global) invites people from all walks of life to make similar choices in lighting. According to the company,

> Consumer insight recognizes that individuals understand the effects of climate change and want to protect the environment as well as improving their quality of life. However, they do not want to compromise one for the other, and see lighting as a feasible way of using less energy without restricting quality of life.

> Today, long after the Live Earth event, this concept of collective individual choices still drives the growth of their compact fluorescent lightbulbs.

6

Now, suppose you were setting out to make a herd save a billion kilograms of greenhouse gases and purchase three million lightbulbs. How much advertising would you need? How many impressions would each person need to see? Above all, would even the best advertising in the world start a movement flocking in your direction? By flying alongside this gathering crowd and attracting them, Philips became part of a cause and at the same time part of a market.

While even the most successful marketing efforts in the past may have improved sales metrics or won a big award, successful marketing today must become part of a collaborative online consciousness. For example, a recent television spot of ours was downloaded by over a million people from viral video sites – sites that are not controlled by us or any paid promotional entity. As we will see shortly, these human connections hold the power to drive fundamental shifts in consumer preferences, brand identity, and ultimately sales and profitability.

We are not the only ones noticing this change. A recent report from PricewaterhouseCoopers starts by stating, "One consumer voice can morph into a community in minutes," and makes the case that the speed and scale of consumer conversations are now often market-changing.[1] Around the same time, Forrester Research examined the current state of marketing and concluded, as I do, that we must shift from creating messages to nurturing connections with consumers.[2]

The simple premise of this thinking is that we are experiencing an unprecedented human transformation from a herd of individuals to a linked community, and those who succeed in the future must learn to influence this community instead of just selling to members of the herd. It is a time of challenge and change for followers of traditional marketing approaches. At the same time, it represents a fantastic opportunity to have people flock toward your products and services, driven by the energy of the swarm itself.

The anatomy of a swarm

We often think of an individual person as having limited influence. Put a million or so of them together, though, and soon we all create complex social colonies, quickly learning – *as a group* – to optimize our survival and functioning. All by having a leaderless group of agents follow simple rules that range from seeking food to checking our e-mail.

Herds are also homogenous groups that share similar characteristics, but are programmed to meet *individual* goals. Picture a herd of cattle in a field. They have a great deal in common: They all graze, swish their tails, and go "moo." They inhabit the same place and live similar lives. But if you go up to one of these cows and pat it on the nose, feed it, or even jump on its back, nothing changes in the rest of the herd. You have a one-on-one relationship with each member of the herd. Indeed, the popular image of the cowboy revolves around a job description of reining in individual members of a herd of cattle, lasso in hand.

Now, let's replace cows with bees. Suddenly, you are no longer dealing with each bee. You are dealing with an interconnected social organism that behaves as one. No one talks of "herding" bees. You cannot make any individual bee do anything. You can only influence the entire swarm, just like when you walk toward a field of birds and watch them take flight in unison.

Swarms of humans in the marketplace have minds of their own as well. For example, how did you plan your last vacation? If you are like many people, you research your destination through online resources on the Internet. You shop for the lowest airfare on an interactive travel site, as airlines adjust their fares in real time based on the demand cycle you are now part of. You compare hotel ratings on consumer travel websites, and then after the trip you share your experience by posting your own thoughts. In other words, you follow simple rules of your own, interacting with a living environment of people and businesses who are, in turn, reacting to you. Trying to influence you as an individual against this wealth of constantly evolving knowledge would be like trying to drink from a fire hose.

Even as recently as the late twentieth century, you approached the same process very differently. You saw a nice ad on television, or looked at brochures at a travel agency, and made your purchase. You were part of many one-to-one transactions that went no further than you, your television, your immediate community, and the brand images of the airlines, hotels, and destinations you chose. You had no way of knowing what a vacationer from Vancouver or a salesperson from Singapore thought of the products and services you bought. And the experience you had was of no more account to the world than a tree falling deep in the middle of a vast forest.

Today, you are part of a community of agents, and its simple rules are not much different from the rules that drive a school of fish. It wasn't always that way: Many of us inhabited a fairly self-contained world revolving around the small cocoons of our neighborhoods, our workplaces, and above all our households, all bathed in the glow of traditional mass media. Today, digital connectivity has shattered this world forever, and we all react in real time to the signals that this virtual world creates within itself.

The Facebook effect

Started as a way for college students to keep in touch with each other in cyberspace, Facebook has quickly grown to become synonymous with the concept of social networking. Today less than a third of its more than 35 million users are on campus, and its founder Mark Zuckerberg has reportedly turned down repeated offers to purchase his operation for billions of US dollars. Some analysts have valued the company at more than US$10 billion, which would give Facebook almost twice the value generated by the sale of *The Wall Street Journal* – more than 100 years its senior.

What has boosted Facebook from an online community to a social phenomenon is how it was designed to accommodate interactive "apps" that share videos, automatically pulse your network of friends with questions, or communicate information across your community. Third parties are free to develop these applications, and their impact on the way people connect has been dubbed the "Facebook effect."

9

Today the average user spends nearly 20 minutes per day using Facebook.

According to Zuckerberg, Facebook automates the "social graph" that has always connected people, in the real world or cyberspace, and his goal is nothing less than to make his application the hub of people's online social activity. With adults forming the single largest demographic joining the service nowadays, it is quickly becoming a model for how a swarm of people interact within a virtual community.

Peers and predators: influencing a community

Marketing is fundamentally a matter of influence and identity. While influencing people and building a brand image have traditionally involved one-way communication from sellers to buyers, digital communities represent a consistent "group think" that is constantly in motion. In this brave new world, social behavior now revolves around flocking or fleeing, and how you are perceived. One of the most critical areas is your relationship to this online society: In other words, are you seen as a predator or as a peer?

If you are a peer, you have credibility and influence, and people begin to flock to you. When they trust your brand *and* you are attracting the members of the social network, your own marketing efforts quickly multiply and spread beyond the borders of your own efforts.

Take the example of Knut the polar bear that was mentioned earlier. We did not just toss this bear cub a bright red ball, snap a few pictures, and wait for the tourists to come flocking to Canada. Our subsidiary Radar DDB, a social marketing agency in Canada, oversaw a promotional effort that caught the ear of influential media, blogs, and social networks.

We calculated the equivalent marketing value of the exposure we received at nearly a third of a million dollars. But the community itself ultimately took it from there and spread the word far and wide.

This was a case where our efforts did not look a lot like traditional marketing, although it was still a lot of hard work. But by shifting the focus from advertising response to engaging a community, we get a response that is far out of proportion to our efforts.

Once the digital community treats you as a peer, this kind of nonlinear response can become normal or even expected. Later in this book, we will examine some examples of what happens when strong brands take the next step and engage their communities; for example, why nearly two-thirds of us now search the Internet on Google; or, how 30-second cartoon summaries of major movies spread through cyberspace to help Volkswagen build a brand identity and a market leadership position for one of its cars.

Conversely, if you are perceived as a predator by the community, people will flee from your brand. Ask any business that has had its service quality or labor practices challenged by websites and viral videos, for example, and it will tell you that no amount of public relations can overcome the impact of the community itself – serving as judge, jury, and executioner – reacting to the perception of its members. Similarly, there is no silencing the voice of consumer opinions on your products and services. The reality of how you connect with your brand – good, bad, and ugly – is there for all to see.

This means that today, more than ever, you cannot fake a brand. Your authenticity is everything, and the community has truly become a modern-day big brother that watches over you. While you can lead a herd, you cannot lead a swarm – but you can influence them, in one of three ways:

Conviction: Behind every brand is a great idea. All brands start in the same place, with the personal vision and conviction of the marketers behind them.

Collaboration: In the old days, marketing was something you added onto your product. Nowadays, you must be part of the community and vice versa: You have to give them a voice in what you do, and perhaps even link them with each other. This means that your marketing must now reach all the way back to the innermost levels of your business.

Creativity: Creativity represents one element that remains constant in our efforts to connect with people, regardless of what media we use. In an era of digital connectivity, our creativity must evolve beyond the skills of attracting individuals, toward new ways of reaching communities and their points of influence.

Each of these terms has timeless origins, but they now have very specific and evolving meanings in an on-demand, 24/7 world of interconnected consumers. As we explore each of these in more detail throughout the book, you will see that they paint a picture of a world where marketing as we know it must change. You will discover a world where core brand values are now becoming more central than ever – and, more important, a world where we must shift from targeting individuals to engaging communities.

The Dartmouth Green:
The campus square that designed itself

The Dartmouth Green is a large grass-covered quadrangle that serves as the physical and emotional center of Dartmouth College, a well-known Ivy League university. It consists of a grass field crossed by seven gravel walking paths that were not designed by any architect or planner, but rather by Dartmouth students themselves – and they did not even know it!

When these paths were last adjusted in 1931, the design goal was to reflect the natural walking paths of students as accurately as possible, so Dartmouth came up with a novel idea to create their layout. Being located in Hanover, New Hampshire, there is no lack of snow at Dartmouth. So one snowy morning, as the rush to and from classes took place, school representatives observed what footpaths were naturally worn into the blanket of white between buildings. These footpaths ultimately became the blueprint for the actual paths that now traverse the Green.

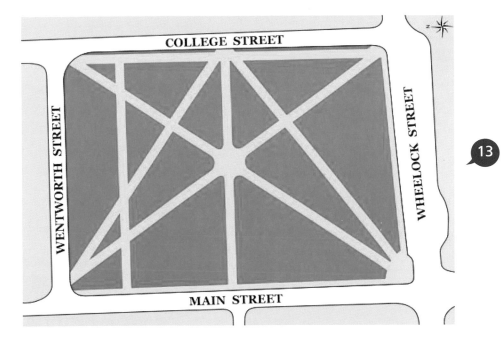

Layout of the footpaths on the Green at Dartmouth College.

From consumers to communities

Many great things have emerged from the efforts of individual human beings, but it is now becoming clear to both scientists and thought leaders that the truly life-changing ideas of our era – ranging from participatory democracy to the Internet – emerged from the behavior of groups. No one imagined things like eBay, Facebook, or e-commerce years ago when the Internet protocol was first conceived, nor did the founding fathers of the United States decide what the Social Security system or copyright laws would look like when they drafted the Constitution. All of these things emerged from the actions of millions of people over time. More important, each of them involved great ideas from small groups that eventually spread through and changed the course of the United States.

This view is changing the way we look at people as consumers, of both products and ideas. For example, a decade ago people started to talk about viral or "buzz" marketing. Popularized in metaphors such as the game Six Degrees of Separation, we looked at how any person is connected to any other person by six or fewer connections – and, more important, how each person influences a network of people, who in turn influence their network in a rapidly accelerating web of connectivity. This viral view of consumers, intensified by the growth of social networking and the Internet, has changed the way we interact with each other, and the way we perceive and purchase products.

Today we are starting to see a much broader view of the world than the viral one. Both real and virtual viruses spread from person to person, but we are discovering that there are larger and more important factors that influence an entire marketplace, in the same way that a flock of birds deftly and instinctively flies around a tree. Instead of just creating a buzz where individuals say "psst" to each other, we have the power to tap into the behavior of the entire community. You see it when groups react to their environment by suddenly starting to wear the latest fashion, or banding together to form a social movement. People are now emerging as the higher life form behind the networks where viral communication takes place – and in the process, have become the new media.

Running this out to more recent trends such as social networks, Web 2.0, and influencers, I see a similar pattern. All of these are important enabling tools for reaching social networks. But they are just that – tools. Engaging a swarm, which may involve any or none of these tools, is the larger direction that lies underneath all of these trends. Therefore, before you think about creating branded content or marketing on Facebook, I want you to first start thinking about a much larger objective: creating a community around your brand.

We see this growing move toward these types of communities every day, not just through the eyes of brands and consumers, but in the rhythm of our own lives. Here at DDB, we ourselves are an interconnected community. With 13,000 employees in offices all over the world, the creative ideas that drive our daily business flow through our organization as a constant digital stream of communication, which in turn informs the organizational culture that flows back toward them. A single project might involve input from our social marketing agency group, our interactive group, and our Hispanic marketing group, among many others. They function interdependently, turning like a school of fish within the medium of a high-intensity, creative workplace. This evolution of our own social network reminds us that society itself is changing, and we must change with it.

So now, come with me on a journey into a brand new way of thinking about your market. It is a trek that will take you from targeting individuals to influencing social networks of consumers that can reach into the millions or even billions. Along the way, we will look at what makes virtual communities tick, and how to navigate in an age of digital connectivity.

15

We will see how core values of conviction, collaboration, and creativity will let you be a peer and a partner with these groups. Finally, we will look at how new ways of marketing can engage these communities, and what it will mean for your organization.

Years ago, people used to say that marketing was all about the consumer. We are now starting to discover that we only had it half right – it is also about communities. In the rest of this book, we are going to take a deeper look into this new and highly connected world, and how that is changing the way we look at selling products and ideas.

The Anatomy of a Digital Community

Ants are not the smartest creatures in the world.

The life of an individual ant is a very simple one: It basically searches for food and follows the scents other ants leave behind. You can even simulate the behavior of one pretty accurately on a computer.

Individual ants are not very intelligent, but a colony of ants is. When you put a million or so of them together, they quickly locate the shortest paths to resources, they form complex and efficient superhighways to get to these resources, and they adapt to changes in their environment. They even use their bodies to build bridges over obstacles during high traffic periods, and then disperse afterward. They have a collective intelligence that lets them flock to resources or flee from danger.[1]

Humans also behave differently when we congregate in groups. We band people together around a dream to go to the moon, and a decade later put our footprints there. One day we are individuals complaining about our government, and the next day we are a crowd of thousands tearing down the Berlin Wall. And perhaps most important for this era, we are responding to the next generation of the web by forming social networks.

I would make the case that this tendency to form groups is accelerating: We are becoming a global community linked by these digital social networks. In the process, we are behaving in exactly the same ways as swarms in nature do.

According to statistics from Tribal DDB, over 80 percent of students *and* 80 percent of professionals currently use social networking sites.

Forty percent of these people post to them at least weekly. Even more telling is that over one-third of humankind now has access to wireless technology, ranging from phones to the Internet. People turn to these networks in the same way that ants follow their scents, and there is a growing case that animal swarm behaviors track very closely with how humans now behave in this era of global connectivity.

This kind of behavior is not a new development for human beings, but rather our natural state of being. Juxtaposed with the perspective of thousands of years, the modern view of humans as a herd of isolated families is a very recent cultural phenomenon, and in a real sense social networks are leading us back to the roots of our evolutionary nature. This is why marketing at the level of linked communities is not a fad, but rather a direction that is an inevitable part of our evolution as a society.

According to biologists such as Princeton University's Dr. Iain Couzin, communities of living things can be seen in terms of five key principles: they follow simple rules, develop a collective intelligence, respond quickly to small changes, are self-reinforcing, and respond quickly as a group. Let's look at how these principles apply to people in a Web 2.0 era, and what I believe they will mean for the future of brands.

Digital communities follow simple rules

We humans tend to think of ourselves as rugged individuals who climb mountains, read Shakespeare, and drink fine wines. But we are amazingly predictable from a biologist's viewpoint. We seek sources of food, try to get on the shortest line, or keep an appropriate amount of personal space around ourselves in a crowd.

Like other species, we follow simple rules with multiple variables. For example, we tend to eat what is in front of us, even when we aren't hungry: Cornell University researcher Brian Wansink even did a study where he served people stale popcorn after a full dinner, and found that they consumed more than 200 calories of it per person.[2] And people in the marketing field have done extensive research on the simple rules that form the aggregate behavior of consumers.

Our tendency to follow rules, often unspoken, has become even sharper as we flock to online networks. We look up people on Google after we meet them. We check to see what other people think about products and services before we buy them. Most important, many of us can't resist adding our own experiences to the dialogue. The more information out there, the stronger we are drawn toward it.

What does this kind of predictability mean for your brand? It means that we have to know what attracts people – whether it be fun, comfort, safety, accomplishment, or something else motivating our particular audience – and make that part of the relationship between them and our brands, so that they congregate in our direction as they follow their own simple rules.

In marketing, we sometimes have a fantasy that we can change the rules the masses follow. If we create the perfect ad or the perfect campaign, people will flock to our brand. Then we run into the reality that we are just one voice among many now, and as loud as we try to make it, we still can't pull people away from the influence of other voices.

19

Using simple rules to conquer your campus

At least one group is painting college life as a time where people learn from each other, make friends with a wide range of new people – and then go to war with them online and conquer them.

Go Cross Campus (www.goxcampus.com) is a massive multiplayer game designed to pit groups against each other across a college campus using object-centered social networking. Groups of players are assigned armies and given a set of simple rules to attack other armies, defend their position, or conquer territory. They can meet online and offline to strategize, and the goal of the game is to completely take over your campus.

The game is designed to take less than two minutes a day for participants to play, and yet its rules allow a wide range of strategic moves, including impeaching commanders and capturing spies. Today nearly 35,000 participants have commanded over two million armies and issued more than 12 million orders.

While currently aimed at college students, the game site is planning to expand to other organizations such as workplaces in the near future, and a game based on a map of the UK and US television show "The Office" is currently underway. In the meantime, games like this serve as just one example of turning a community loose around a set of simple rules and creating an outcome.

20

Digital communities have a collective intelligence

The great psychologist Carl Jung spoke of people having a "collective unconscious," where we retain the memory of what we have learned in past generations. More recently, modern biologists have shown that human communities maintain their collective intelligence through artifacts they create for themselves. In both cases, we carry the seeds of our own history genetically and preserve it.

Look at our own network of roads, for example. In the United Kingdom, some roads date back to the early Romans, while the British motorway system is an artifact of modern car travel. The former adapted to life thousands of years ago, while the latter reflects the past century. Both coexist today as a continuum of evolution.

A digital community deposits its intelligence online in forms ranging from blog entries to product ratings. You see its collective intelligence in the form of an instant online poll or the emergence of marketplaces like eBay. More important, you can see it in how we create the structures of our own social networks. They are today's digital equivalent of the Roman road systems.

Today this collective intelligence has changed our own social infrastructure. People purchase products and services as members of a community. They have *always* done so: Generations ago, and even hundreds of years ago, we consulted our families, friends, and neighbors about their brand preferences. Now we function as part of a larger social network whose collective intelligence spans the depths of cyberspace. This is the world we must engage in the marketing approaches of the future.

Digital communities respond quickly to small changes

Did you know that in the United States, it only takes about 1 percent of our population – about three million people – to start a social or business movement?[3] According to researchers, the larger a community gets, the smaller a percentage of its members is needed to influence it. Now that we are more connected than ever, the speed at which these small groups can influence people continues to increase as well.

This implies that we have to start thinking about social influencers as well as mass markets. Traditional marketing thinking has always been to reach small percentages of a large population group. Why not expand this brute-force perspective to one where we attract and influence the "scouts" who can in turn influence the rest of us? The customers who post their opinions online, the bloggers, and the early adopters all play

21

a role in linking us to communities – and more importantly, membership in this fraternity of influencers is now as close as someone's Internet connection.

Hula hoops:
An early viral phenomenon

For close to 3,000 years, children around the world have twirled around inside of hoops for play and exercise. But in 1958 inventors Richard Knerr and Arthur "Spud" Melin, founders of the Wham-O toy company, perfected a plastic version of this hoop and set the world on fire.

Their marketing approach was simple: Give them away to targeted school children in conjunction with national advertising and retail distribution. Within two years, sales of Wham-O's Hula Hoop® exceeded 100 million, and hula hoops became one of the signature examples of a viral fad that spread through a population.

As with many fads, the hula hoop craze eventually died down, as Wham-O – already a successful firm on the strength of its Frisbee flying disc – moved on to creating other new products such as the SuperBall® and the Hacky Sack®. But the original Hula Hoop has since had several successful revivals through engaging new consumers, such as the exercise craze of the 1980s and the two-million-participant World Hula Hoop Championships. Today it remains one of Wham-O's flagship products, and people still continue to set endurance records for using them.

(*Sources*: www.whamo.com, Richard Knerr [obituary], *The Times* (UK), Jan. 18, 2008, Wikipedia.)

As we become a human digital swarm, we are becoming sensitive to small changes in general, particularly when these changes stand out. Mathematicians refer to this phenomenon as the "gradient" or rate of change, and we are all inherently sensitive to gradients. For example, look at how a viral video or blog entry spreads like wildfire through a swarm of people, or how the word about a new product can erupt seemingly overnight.

The good news here is that in an era of swarm marketing, it doesn't always take much of a response to send people flocking toward your brand. Take the Apple iPod, for example – it rose almost overnight not only to dominate the market for portable music players but also to fundamentally change the way we purchase music. Today many music collections, including mine, are stored on a device that fits in our pockets.

The bad news is that it doesn't take much to send them away either; digital communities can quickly flee in much the same way that a school of fish will dart away from a predator – and for much the same reason. This is why some brands fail catastrophically; for example, the bankruptcy of many large firms is almost always preceded by a precipitous drop in sales. As the connectivity of humans continues to increase, I feel that we will need to focus on the "gradients" of our own brands more urgently than ever.

23

Digital communities are self-reinforcing

Look at the way most of us purchase life insurance or set up a bank account. The majority of us don't research every bank or insurance company. Instead, we talk to our friends or our families – or increasingly, resources on the Internet – and then we pick a company and stick with it for life.

This kind of self-reinforcing behavior reflects the way animal colonies react toward things like food sources, and the same thing is happening as swarms flock toward brands. For example, my hometown of Louisville, Kentucky, has a famous local dish called a "Hot Brown," an open-faced turkey sandwich in a thick cheese sauce that the Brown Hotel created as an experiment in 1920. Despite a wide range of menu items, the Hot Brown soon became the choice of 95 percent of its diners.

The Hot Brown is a good example of the biologist's argument that a swarm will tip precipitously to one of several alternatives: 75 years later, it remains the Brown Hotel's signature dish. We can see the same thing throughout human history. Do you know why screws tighten clockwise instead of counterclockwise? They could have just as easily gone either way, but human consciousness tipped in the direction of going clockwise, and we have never changed since.

What this means for marketing is that you can't just have a better product or better advertising. Your brand needs to influence people in its direction, particularly at those critical points where people make brand decisions. In an era of social networking, this means influencing those people who leave information behind as artifacts for the rest of the crowd – in other words, those most vocal consumers who leave their opinions online for others to see.

It also means that while every consumer is important, there are critical points at which we need to engage these consumers. There are critical points where fundamental patterns of behavior are established, whether it is choosing your bank or establishing your role in a social group, after which the perceived costs of exploration become too high. I would also extend this argument to the ecosystem of social networking itself: Once someone establishes structures like Facebook or Amazon.com, for example, it becomes that much harder to dislodge them.

This doesn't necessarily mean that one has to be first to market. It does mean that we need to think past the technical advantages of our products and services, into the realm of how we engage both early adopters and new customers. Above all, it means that we must think like the rest of our fellow humans as they first join the community.

Betamax versus VHS: A community tipping point

What makes a product become a dominant brand? Is it being first to market? Or having higher quality? Or having the weight of a major organization behind it?

The Betamax standard for home videotape recording had all of these things going for it, and yet it became a classic marketing case study of a product that consumers eventually fled from.

At the dawn of personal videocassette recorders (VCRs) in the mid-1970s, Sony's Betamax represented a revolution for consumers: Using a tape cartridge that was smaller than a paperback book, people could suddenly record live television in their homes and play it back later.

While Betamax essentially had the market for VCRs to itself in 1975, it was soon challenged by the competing VHS format developed by Japan Victor Corporation. Sony and JVC executives had earlier been unable to compromise on a common format and brought competing products to market, and despite the technical superiority of Sony's format, VHS soon outsold it by a three-to-one margin within six years.

So what killed Betamax, if it wasn't its quality? In a very real sense, American football. When American firm RCA decided to OEM a videocassette recorder for the US market, it insisted that the product be able to record the four-hour length of an entire football game. Sony engineers balked

25

for fear of degrading picture quality, while JVC's parent company Matsushita agreed to this request, and the rest is history.

While both products remained on the market for many years, VHS won out because consumers strongly preferred longer recording times and cheaper cassettes. Today Betamax versus VHS stands as a classic example of what happens when a company listens to its engineers instead of its customers.

(*Source*: Wikipedia contributors, "Videotape Format War," Feb. 22, 2008.)

Digital communities respond quickly as a group

As anyone who has ever had the misfortune of stepping in a nest of stinging insects can confirm, communities of living things react quickly as a single organism. More important, they can change their own state very quickly.

I would take both of these arguments a step further and say that human beings have both changed state and shifted toward speed with the advent of Web 2.0 and social networks. We once sat in front of our televisions and socialized in small groups. Today we share information with everyone in our MySpace network or our blog feed, and each of these people then passes it on to their own networks. For example, when we release a viral video for a client that engages consumers, it often reaches a million people or more for a tiny fraction of the cost of traditional advertising. It is here, in its quick response to small inputs that the behavior of a digital community parts ways with traditional marketing thought.

What do these rules tell us about marketing? That human beings respond in predictable ways when they are in groups. Moreover, the closer we get to linking ourselves digitally, the more our behavior resembles things like animal swarms and human armies. So when digital social networks facilitate our response as a group, our behavior does not so much reflect technological advancement as it does a return to nature.

This, in turn, means that we must start thinking more like a community to effectively market to them. We must look at how communities of people follow simple rules, have collective intelligence, can be influenced, respond to small changes, quickly settle on one alternative, and move fast. It means that we will perhaps have as much to learn from science as from advertising in the future. Above all, it means that we are facing a world of people who now must be seen as a collective whole, and not just as a herd of individual consumers.

The emergence of emergence

Who designed the skyline of your city?

The answer is, probably no one. In most cities of the world, individual organizations create individual buildings at different periods, creating a mosaic that becomes the visual image of where we live. Some of these buildings stand out, like the Eiffel Tower in Paris, while others blend as part of the vastness of places like metropolitan Tokyo or midtown Manhattan. But no one person sat down one day to plan what these urban landscapes would look like.

This is called *emergence*, where a whole is created that is greater than the individual parts that form it. You see it in the form of the ant colonies or termite "cathedrals" that spring forth from the labors of social networks in nature. In human history, you can see its footprints in concepts such as participatory democracy. No one decided what the specifics of copyright law or public health programs would look like when

27

the United States was founded over 200 years ago, but by creating a system of government, we turned loose the power of our votes to create all of these other structures.

The Internet era is a very high-speed example of emergence, with a "skyline" ranging from e-commerce to social networking that was created in barely more than a decade, yet plays a central role in how we live, work, and play. I can't imagine life without my BlackBerry nowadays, and don't even stop to think that years ago I once communicated with the same pens, paper, and postage stamps my parents' generation used. It is not only this high connectivity but also *the rate at which it is changing* that is making us behave more organically.

Emergence does not always have pleasant consequences, in animals or in people. In the animal kingdom, it can mean the Darwinism of eating or being eaten. With a digital society, it can mean being flooded with undesirable information. In the early days of the Internet, for example, many online communities were quickly flooded by spammers trying to sell products or boost the search engine rankings of their websites. Soon many of them became unreadable, with legitimate information buried under hundreds or thousands of unrelated posts.

However, even situations like these lead us to a more important point: The collective intelligence of a linked social group adapts and evolves. Today most of these message boards have safeguards to keep automated spam out, and eventually this "validation" model of building an online community helped to build the roots of social networking.

This in turn leads us to the place we are now: a world where a structure has emerged for how we communicate online, and in the process became a community. A community that is as global as the Internet and as specific as a message board for quilting enthusiasts. A community that has quickly evolved throughout the first decade of the new millenium and will evolve even further over the next one.

The key principle about emergence is that when you turn a community of independent agents loose, structures emerge. When you create a particular type of government, a society and its laws form around it. When you create the Internet, structures ranging from e-commerce to Wikipedia suddenly sprout and take root in our lives. And when you unleash the personal connectivity of Web 2.0, we become a world where the voice of one person can suddenly multiply across an entire population. It is in this new environment that we will live and function from now on, and it will not stop here.

A social network for building social networks

What happens to social networks when they make it easy for people to create more social networks?

This describes the business model for Ning, a Silicon Valley company that markets an infrastructure for creating social networks, whose members in turn can easily create other networks. With groups ranging from Saturn drivers to fans of the band Good Charlotte, Ning represents a platform where people can quickly build a community with forums, photos and videos, message boards, and individual member pages – and these members can in turn create and link to social networks of their own.

Ning refers to this model as a "viral expansion loop," and it is a road they have traveled before – cofounder Marc Andreessen helped usher in the Mosaic browser that soon had everyone creating and reading Web pages in the 1990s, while CEO Gina Bianchini's roots came from the dot-com boom. Its growth, from 60,000 networks in mid-2007 to nearly a quarter-million a year later, reflects the exponential nature of networks expanding to other

29

networks. The emergence of tools such as Ning serves as an example of how communities can not only grow, but grow more communities.

Source: Penenberg, Adam L., "Ning's Infinite Ambition," *Fast Company* magazine, May 2008.

From Revere to refrigerators: calling communities to action

Students of American history often point to the ride of patriot Paul Revere, who hopped on his horse in the middle of the night to warn people that British troops were advancing. This ride was immortalized in a poem by Longfellow that symbolized the rugged individualism of early Americans who helped fight oppression.

The real story behind this ride is a little different, however. In reality, Revere and two other riders set out on different paths and got other people to start spreading the word – including hanging lanterns in a church that spurred an entire town to action – and before long, according to historians, there were as many as 40 people spreading the word on horseback.

What is romanticized in popular culture as a single heroic act is, in reality, an early example of seeding information at a community level. You had information being passed from person to person and spreading, much like today's viral marketing techniques. You also had information posted in places where large numbers of people could see it, such as the church lantern, perhaps much like we deposit information in online social networks. Finally, people responded collectively to a wave of information spread by a few people, and defeated the British.

Now fast-forward to a campaign we recently did for our client Brastemp, one of Brazil's largest appliance manufacturers. Like Paul Revere, we set out to create a message and send it out to influencers who then spread this message for us, instead of simply advertising a product.

Appliances such as refrigerators, washers, and dryers have always had a very functional image, based around features and capabilities. These are important, but flocks of consumers are not solely drawn by which refrigerator uses how many BTUs this particular month. So our challenge was to create an emotional connection with Brastemp and its products, one that would represent both its design philosophy and its attraction to the swarm: a sense of authenticity that would differentiate us from a sea of similar product claims.

First, we studied what authenticity meant to people, using techniques ranging from anthropological research to blog surveys and focus groups. Our conclusion was that people saw the world in terms of what we called an "A side" – in other words, what they had to do in life – and a "B side" that held the possibility of being able to do whatever one wants to do at any given time. The concept of a "B side" was already well established in Brazil as an analogy to the other side of a music record, as a metaphor for the more laid-back side of life: those spontaneous, authentic, pleasurable moments of life that are ours to control.

31

The attitude then became a design philosophy for Brastemp, with products and features aimed at enhancing the "B side" of life: refrigerators that dispensed cans and frosted glasses for party lovers, a mini washing machine for the bathroom designed for lingerie, and microwaves with a memory button to save your favorite recipe.

We then targeted influencers to establish Brastemp appliances as supporting the "B Side" of life. For example, we held events for opinion makers in Brazilian cities together with the country's largest publishing house, depicting kitchens, lofts, and laundries decorated by renowned architects around "B side" themes. We held contests for chefs to compete for the best "B side" recipes. We sponsored a regular three-minute television program portraying the "B sides" of leading Brazilians. And we even created a website that encouraged people to share their own "B sides" with each other. The result was an impressive 11 percent increase in sales in a consolidated market.

What is more important is what we *didn't* do. We didn't just take out a big ad for an appliance and hope that some people would go out and buy one. Instead, we targeted points of influence, ranging from the press to chefs to thought leaders. We gave them something they valued and *they* spread our message, like Paul Revere and his riders; for example, the number of blog posts in Brazil titled "B side" increased by 400 percent

An image from the Brastemp "B Side" campaign in Brazil.
Reproduced with permission from Brastemp and Deluxe Photo, Brazil.

during this campaign. This is an example of standing herd marketing on its head and engaging a community.

So what does this mean for you?

What does the growth of a digital society ultimately mean for *your* brand? The short answer is that we are already in a new world that has moved from targeting herds to influencing groups. This is a world where connecting with the right few people can send millions more flocking to you. And a world where, more than ever, the integrity and engagement of your brand means as much as the ways you promote it.

Throughout this book, I am going to present some very specific ideas for influencing the new digital community we live in. They will not be quick fixes, but rather some fresh new insights that I feel will stand the test of time. For example, I don't know if we should be advertising on social networking sites five years from now, but I do know that you will need to build a community around your brand. These and many other principles are becoming the new currency of marketing.

I am also going to take you on a journey of discovery that will lead you to ask some questions of your own, because we don't know all of the answers yet. At the same time, research has already taught us a valuable lesson about where we are heading, as both consumers and as a culture. If you don't believe that we are becoming a digitally linked community, go spend an evening on MySpace and see how many friends people have – or visit YouTube and look at how many people are viewing, commenting on, and spreading viral videos. More important, look at how your own relationship to brands has changed over the past decade.

I do not use the term evolution lightly, because my friends in biology use it to describe a process that takes place over generations if not centuries, but we are watching a real evolution in the way people think and socialize. For example, a recent class project by Professor Michael

Wesch at Kansas State University showed that a typical student reads only eight books a year, but 2,300 web pages and over 1,200 Facebook profiles. They write 42 pages of content for their classes, but more than 500 pages of e-mail for their friends. Our next generation will spend a large percentage of their life tightly linked with a network of peers that reaches around the globe.[4]

This kind of fundamental social change is why I believe so passionately in the power of community. Herd marketing is not going away anytime soon. The return on investment for traditional marketing is still very much there. But we must take a fresh look at how communities behave, what makes them flock or flee, and, more importantly, their relationship to brands and purchasing behavior. In my view, influencing these communities represents the higher purpose of marketing, and will create powerful leverage for strong brands.

Welcome to the Age of Reference, Not Deference

This past century was a great time to be in my profession of advertising.

It was great because we had more power to influence people than any other business on the face of the Earth. We could take a product, create a message around it, and attract consumers to it. We turned products into brands, and brands into icons. It was as though we were given a set of magical superpowers.

Take American Tourister, for example. They made quality luggage that was designed for the rigors of travel. But it wasn't until 1969, when we launched an advertising campaign that featured an 800-pound gorilla named Otto throwing a piece of its luggage around a cage and jumping on it, that it became a brand that everyone *automatically associated in their minds* with being tough. Nearly 40 years later, that gorilla is still part of the brand identity of American Tourister and its current parent company, Samsonite.

Or take the Volkswagen Beetle of 1959. Back then, America lived in a post–World War II world where bigger was better, fuel economy was for sissies, and V8 engines were a status symbol. So how do you promote a little car with an air-cooled engine from former archrival Germany? In our case, by creating a social movement.

Our "Think Small" campaign, which featured a small black-and-white Beetle and extolled the virtues of getting 32 miles per gallon, paying

The 1959 Volkswagen "Think Small" campaign.

Reproduced with permission from Volkswagen USA.

less for repair bills, and squeezing into tiny parking spaces, didn't just sell a product. It was a creative dialogue that spoke back to an era of conspicuous consumption – and in the process, it became a campaign that *Advertising Age* rated as the best of the past century.

In fact, we weren't just selling products: We were changing the world. Another advertisement we did, showing a little girl picking a daisy as a nuclear mushroom cloud erupted behind her, played a role in the US presidential election of Lyndon Johnson. Decades later, at the dawn of a new millennium, we still held sway over public opinion, with over US$300 billion per year in global annual advertising revenue. It was a time when image sold products and ideas, and as advertising professionals *we* got to create these images. It was truly a great time in our business.

Here is why I feel today is an even greater time. The human digital community is fundamentally changing marketing because instead of just relying on authority figures, "expert sources," mainstream media and mass advertising, people are also relying on members of their social network – such as friends, family, peers, and fellow online community members – to guide their decisions.

At first glance, this does not sound like the happiest statement for people in advertising. It sounds like we are losing the magical powers we once had to create images and brands. If we create a fantastic brand identity for a product and people still rate it poorly on the Internet, the people will win and we cannot do anything about it. We have now entered into a new and more collaborative phase of marketing, one that is truly a conversation with consumers as a whole.

In my view, however, this is great news. Why? Because brands that engage communities can far outperform those who are still speaking to the herd: This is why companies like Google and Facebook have accomplished the same kind of market capitalization over the past five years that some

37

of our most cherished brands have built over a century. This trend will move marketing from our comfortable, traditional niche to a much bigger and brighter world: one built around sustainable brand communities that flock toward us in response to very small efforts. What we have seen so far is just the tip of the iceberg.

The key to this change is that you and your marketing are now just one voice in the collective intelligence of this community. Its members speak to each other and listen to each other. If your brand can engage and influence them you have tremendous leverage, and if it chases them away no amount of marketing will get them back. We are entering an age of reference, not deference.

How Web 2.0 is leading to People 2.0

We are in the most interconnected generation in history. But it is not just digital technology that has changed us from a herd of consumers to a community of connected human beings. It is a process of social change. The social networks of Web 2.0 have created a new human mind-set that I call People 2.0: a society that has moved from isolated bedrooms, cubicles, and classrooms to a flock that fundamentally thinks differently – and moreover, thinks as a group.

I see three things that set this new society apart from the way we once were:

1. Privacy is turning into community
The Chinese language reportedly has no word for "privacy" in the Western sense of the word.[1] Increasingly, the digital swarm we inhabit is also devaluing privacy.

Part of this change is generational. I grew up in a generation whose parents used to criticize our rock music and long hair. Now that we are the parents of teenagers, some of us find ourselves similarly dumbfounded about a generation that records even the most personal and intimate aspects of their lives on blogs and MySpace pages.

Another part of this change is digital. Once upon a time we wrote letters meant to be seen by one person, and viewed programs on television that would never be watched again. Today both we and society leave electronic footprints behind us wherever we tread. When you are in the news, get a new job, publish an article, or network with people on LinkedIn, pieces of your life become part of a sea of information and stay there for good.

A third and larger part of this change is social. We *choose* to put very intimate parts of ourselves out in cyberspace. We share recipes, rate products on Amazon.com, talk about our recent breakup on Facebook, and start political movements through viral networking. We make a thoughtful choice to connect with people we may never see, putting large parts of our lives online for all to see: likes, dislikes, wants, needs, and good or bad experiences. These bits of information then become part of a greater whole that we ourselves follow.

Perhaps the most important part of this change is that it is inevitable. As we have emerged from the isolated family cocoons of the post–World War II baby boom we have become more like a flock of birds guided and influenced by each other. We are now willing to share more of ourselves to become part of a greater whole. The result is a global, open-access community that we all belong to.

39

Giving a new meaning to "media exposure"

How do you market traditional underwear to the Internet generation? In the case of Jockey International, the answer took the form of a challenge aimed specifically at the kinds of people who share their lives online: Send us a video of yourself dancing in your skivvies (or, more specifically, *their* skivvies).

Their website jockeyunderwars.com, designed by the Minneapolis-based Periscope agency, pits a group of 64 entrants against each other in head-to-head competition. Website visitors vote on their favorite videos featuring guys, gals, and teams doing PG-rated dance routines in their Jockey underwear, with the winner taking away a US$5,000 prize. With a message board for comments and links to "challenge an underbuddy," the response was great enough for Jockey to launch a second round of competition in early 2008.

While Jockey International is over 125 years old, viral marketing is in fact part of its early history, dating back to a 1930s display of their first briefs in a Chicago department store window on a mid-winter day. The store felt it was inappropriate for the season, but before they could take it down, several hundred pairs had sold. Jockey was soon flying a "Mascu-liner" plane from city to city stocking stores to meet the demand. Today they are using the web and viral marketing to build a registered community of customers in addition to their traditional marketing channels.

2. We all have a lot more leverage

Do you remember the old truism that a happy customer will tell four people about their experience, and an unhappy one will tell eleven people? When you make a customer unhappy today you may be telling the 187 friends signed into his blog feed about it, as well as anyone to whom these 187 people pass his story along, and anyone who searches for your product on Google.

This means that brand experiences are highly contagious. It means that the great vacation someone had at your resort can influence people as fast or faster than your latest advertising campaign – or that the rude receptionist who answers your phone may have just become your chief marketing officer.

These little drops of information that people leave behind – the reviews, the ratings, the blog comments, the connections with each other – become part of an intelligent whole. But perhaps more importantly, the power of *one* person to influence *lots* of people is greater than it ever has been before.

One man's "secret" to a top-ranked blog

Technorati is a well-known website that ranks blog popularity. Out of the 100 million plus blogs tracked, their top 20 include media giants such as AOL's electronic gadget review site Engadget, marketing guru Seth Godin's blog, and the Huffington Post, a news and commentary site whose bloggers include the likes of rocker Patti Smith and news legend Walter Cronkite.

At the same time, not every blog on this list is fronted by a corporation or a celebrity: This top 20 also includes sites like PostSecret, a community art project on a free blog site, where people anonymously mail secrets they have never shared with anyone on handmade postcards. They range from funny (like a scrawled message on a picture of a family in jeans and plaid shirts that the writer "misses when we all matched") to poignant (like the person who wrote that he was too scared to be a father on top of a sonogram). This site, still a one-man operation, currently receives four million visitors per month.

41

3.   Communities maintain their own equilibrium

Over a century ago, psychologists coined the term *gestalt* to describe the state of our experience in the present moment. Digital communities are not just faceless mobs that react to stimuli at the drop of a hat; they are social groups who have their own gestalt, an organizational personality that is unspoken but tangible.

The same thing is true of your own brand community. Try an experiment sometime: Go to a website where consumers can express their opinions about a product or service. Find one that has a really, really bad reputation. See all those negative comments? Now find a brand with an excellent reputation. In all likelihood, it is a love fest.

But here is what is even more interesting: Watch how others react when people make positive comments about brands they hate, or negative comments about brands they love. Either way, people usually go out of their way to defend the aggregate view of the group.

This means that a social network is often not swayed by its loudest voices, but reflects the collective worldview of its individual members. An unhappy customer cannot necessarily destroy your brand with a single click, but if enough people agree with her, she can. All of the advertising in the world cannot change the collective mind of a swarm, but when you create great brand experiences for enough individuals, your advertising can powerfully leverage this same group.

42

Turning around a brand people "hate"

When a company openly admits that many people find its product to be distasteful, how does it keep growing? That was the problem faced by Unilever's Marmite division, a DDB client in the United Kingdom whose 103-year-old flagship product was at a crossroads.

Marmite, manufactured from the byproducts of the beer brewing process, is a vitamin-rich spread with a very strong and acquired taste. Marmite had grown in recent years by embracing its identity as a polarizing food product, around the slogan "You either love it or you hate it." With award-winning television spots showing people running in terror from blobs of Marmite, and separate websites beckoning people who "love" or "hate" the product, it achieved an impressive rate of growth from 1996 to 2002.

But things were changing in the form of flattening sales and demographic roadblocks: consumers were now eating less breakfast at home, bad news for a product that is largely served on toast. And many people in the future market wave of younger consumers were skipping breakfast entirely. So how do you grow a product that doesn't tend to attract new adult consumers?

The answer came from Marmite's own customers, many of whom posted messages and wrote letters asking for a more convenient way to use a gooey, hard-to-spread product that came in a glass jar. Soon the "Squeezy" bottle was born, opening up the product as a sandwich topping and helping existing consumers use more than the average number of jars they purchased a year.

Of course, tradition dies hard with a product that was recently debated in the UK House of Commons as a national icon. *The Guardian* newspaper likened tampering with Marmite's traditional glass jar as being akin to "injecting collagen in the Mona Lisa's lips," and one customer posted that the change would lead to "riots in the street."

But embracing controversy paid off once again for Marmite, with ads including a man with a broken arm struggling with its glass jar, and children's icon Paddington Bear sharing a piece of his sandwich with a choking and gagging pigeon. They even engaged the community with a squeezable Marmite art contest, a feat that would have been near-impossible with the traditional spread. The results were a renewal of the product's strong growth, with an even greater percent increase in sales between 2005 and 2007.

Unilever's Marmite in a new squeezy bottle that expanded its market.

Reproduced with permission from Unilever PLC.

Taken together, all of these signs point to much more than just a change in how we use social networking on the Internet. We are changing as people, in a way that is perhaps more authentic to our being: We are part of a community that is increasingly turning inward rather than outward for guidance. This represents a fundamental shift in our decision-making process. It changes the rules for how we influence this process – and this, in turn, is changing the way we view the process of marketing.

What the age of reference means for marketing

In the old days – the age of deference – marketing was largely a science. You got your message in front of enough people, you measured how many of them responded, you pushed the numbers, turned the crank, and then voilà: People purchased the things you were selling. There is a lot of creativity behind this science, to be sure, but the process fundamentally revolved around you.

Today, in the age of reference, the process revolves around *them*. They seek information, leave information, and decide for themselves what they want to do. And while age-of-deference marketing still can play an important role in building your brand identity and your market share, it has now become one of many voices that vie for attention. To market successfully in the Web 2.0 generation, we now have to become aware of three fundamental rules.

Rule number 1: You can't buy your way into the community's mind-set

In late 2001 singer David Byrne had a tremendous marketing opportunity. His new single "Like Humans Do" was packaged on every new Microsoft Windows XP computer to demonstrate the capabilities of Windows Media Player, exposing the song to millions of computer users at the dawn of digital music. So how well did this song's album sell? It failed to even crack the *Billboard* magazine top 100.

Byrne was not exactly a no-name artist at the time his song was released. As the front man of the Talking Heads, which had a string of critically acclaimed albums in the 1970s and 1980s, his solo work has always had a following. And "Like Humans Do" was not entirely a failure, reaching the top 15 among Internet songs. But the fact that even this massive amount of publicity did not spawn a major hit in the real world underscores what we in advertising have known for a long time: You can't buy influence.

We have seen the same thing happen time and time again in our business. Remember the rash of Super Bowl advertisements for dot-com companies in the year 2000, many of which were for companies that failed soon afterward? This annual sporting event delivers nearly 100 million viewers in the United States and beyond, and remains one of the most coveted advertising spots in our business; but unless you can influence enough of those 100 million people while you have their attention, they will simply pass you by.

Rule number 2: You can't buy your way out of the community's mind-set

Imagine that you hire one of the most powerful advertising agencies on the planet, and spare no expense for advertising and marketing expenses. Then a college student posts a video on YouTube about what a terrible experience she had with your product or service. Or a blogger records a phone call with an indifferent agent in one of your call centers, and his entry gets linked far and wide throughout the blogosphere. Or someone even devotes a website to how terrible your company is, and it gets ranked right up there with your own website in search engine rankings.

Back in the herd marketing days, people like you controlled who heard messages about your brand. Your brand had access to expensive mass media campaigns, and private citizens with an opinion about you did not. Today even the most humble person with an Internet connection can be as powerful a voice for or against your brand as anyone on Madison Avenue.

Just like ants, people today follow simple rules when they are looking for information – and the first place they look isn't always your website or your advertisements. The collective intelligence of the community sustains itself by being open to everyone's input. You often have no control over what they say about you, short of outright libel, and no expenditure of marketing or promotion will muzzle the groupthink that emerges from this community about your brand.

Rule number 3: You can influence the community's mind-set *if* you have a strong brand

With the example we gave earlier about David Byrne, we saw what could happen when you use herd marketing on a large scale with music. Now let's shift gears and compare two musicians who released viral music on the Internet in 2007.

The first was popular alternative band Radiohead, which decided to release its new album *In Rainbows* for Internet download at whatever price fans decided to pay. During the two months it was available under this scheme, it was estimated that over one million fans downloaded a copy. And once it was released as a physical CD *after* these downloads, it shot immediately to number one in the United States and Europe.

The other was a deep-voiced graduate student performing under the name Tay Zonday, whose song "Chocolate Rain" was the number-one viral video on the Internet in 2007. Over 12 million people watched this talented young man's video, many of them downloaded a free MP3 file of the song from his website, and his sudden fame led to television appearances and a host of parodies. As the year came to a close, however, he still lacked a recording deal from a major label.

47

The reason why Radiohead's viral fans made them very successful and Tay Zonday's did not is an important lesson in swarm marketing: *You need a strong brand to influence a community.*

Your brand might have been established through traditional means; for example, Radiohead is a Grammy Award-winning group that sold over 25 million albums from a base of touring and a major recording label contract before they struck out on their own with *In Rainbows*. Or your brand might be new and game-changing, like MySpace and Facebook. Either way, it must connect with the collective groupthink that drives members of the community.

As we walk through this book, I am going to drill down deeper into the three things that I feel create a strong brand in the era of digital communities: conviction, collaboration, and creativity. Radiohead has all three of these things: a musical identity that connects with people, a global fan base that can quickly spread viral information to one another, and a unique idea for distributing their next album. A recent result was one of the most successful releases in history with almost *no* formal marketing effort.

This is exactly what I want to see happen with your brand. You build this brand with your heart, your products, and the right marketing message – and then you use it to create incredibly powerful leverage that attracts and sustains a community of consumers, and that reaches far beyond the effects of traditional marketing. Let's look at how your brand becomes a peer – or a predator – in the eyes of this community, and use this knowledge to engage them in your direction.

Navigating an age of reference

Right now, as you are reading this, somewhere in the world a client company is telling its advertising agency, "Let's do a viral marketing campaign for our product."

The era of viral publicity has arrived with great fanfare. While online marketing expenditures still represent a small fraction of traditional ones, they are growing quicker than any other form of marketing, projected by Forrester Research to increase from US$18.4 billion in 2007 to over $60 billion in five years.[2] If these predictions hold true, online marketing will represent nearly 20 percent of all marketing expenditures. But we are learning that simply spending resources and creating buzz is not enough to create and engage a community.

We live in an era of "new media," but the real new media is not just the web: It is people talking to each other and sharing information. For marketers this represents a sea change. Our relationship with customers is changing from *monologue* to *dialogue* to *conversation*, and the goal for each of us is to become part of that conversation.

The Internet buzz: a tale of two movies

In 2006, the film industry saw an incredible amount of online buzz for a movie in advance of the film *Snakes on a Plane*. Starting with a glowing mention on screenwriter Josh Friedman's blog, the film's campy, high-concept plot (largely explained by the title) soon gave rise to fan sites, song contests, viral videos of mock trailers and film parodies, and an officially sponsored online contest involving entrants posting links on other Internet sites. Distributor New Line Cinema even added five days of reshooting to accommodate feedback from Internet fans.

Unfortunately, the actual performance of the film at the box office never lived up to the hype. While *Snakes on a Plane* did in fact slip into first place for its opening weekend, and ultimately turned a profit, its weak performance and rapid falloff

49

led its studio chief to declare the film a "disappointment." One industry analyst pointed to the results as evidence that heavy Internet users were not necessarily heavy moviegoers.[3] More recently, the monster movie *Cloverfield* used a viral marketing campaign that stirred up people's curiosity about the movie itself. Using a trailer that featured handheld video footage of the destruction of New York City, the name of the movie was never mentioned, just the release date, which also formed the address for the film's prerelease website. Promotional websites offered clues to the story behind the film, viral publicity for specific story elements was launched online, and its cast and crew of relative unknowns were sworn to secrecy regarding the plot. By the time it was released in early 2008, *Cloverfield* set a record for a January film release with a US$43 million gross, nearly three times that of *Snakes on a Plane*.

In our experience, there is a fundamental difference between viral marketing and engaging a community. In the former case, you are often doing traditional marketing in the context of a social network in the hopes that it will spread your message: Instead of running an ad on television, for example, you are setting up a website, a blog, or a page on MySpace. Instead of influencing movie producers for product placement, you are courting influential bloggers and digital pundits. Sometimes it works, and sometimes it does not.

Marketing to a community is more about being where *they* go, offering information or benefits *they* want, and building a relationship with your brand. For example, when the popular virtual world environment Second Life came to Brazil we threw an end-of-year party where we gave away virtual T-shirts, sandals, and bracelets, and got to know people. Later

Dancing the night away at a Second Life party in Brazil hosted by DDB.

we had a New Year's Eve party hosted with our client Philips, and after that a virtual concert with Fatboy Slim that mirrored his real concert in Brazil – including a "live" Q&A with fans afterward in Second Life cyberspace.

51

Did the people who attended these events come because they wanted to learn more about Philips or DDB? More likely, they wanted to have a good time, and when we offered them one they came in droves: In fact, we even had to provide virtual "security" to keep our parties from being overrun by too many avatars. But we succeeded in creating both goodwill and name recognition by starting a relationship with this particular community, many of whom continued to wear our virtual T-shirts in Second Life long after the events were over.

I want to make it clear that we at DDB are fans of effective viral marketing. We are, for that matter, still fans of traditional herd marketing: It serves its function well, and will continue to do so. But our view is that both of these must serve a larger goal, which is to help people find what they are looking for and improve their lives within the context of a community that both seeks and deposits information in real time.

A viral romance

One night on a New York City subway train, web designer Patrick Moberg saw the girl of his dreams. Unfortunately, he couldn't get up the nerve to approach her before she got up and left at her station. So he went home and created a detailed drawing of what she (and he) looked like, added his contact information, and created a web page (nygirlofmydreams. com) asking people to help him find her.

The story and the website spread virally throughout the blogosphere of New York and beyond, until someone noticed a resemblance between the girl in the drawing and an intern at the fashion magazine where he worked: a recent arrival from Australia who was riding the subway after being displaced by an apartment fire. Soon the pieces were put together and the couple had their first date – and an appearance on a national television news show – less than a week after Moberg first posted his website.

As a postscript, Moberg – who ironically worked for a social networking site – took his budding romance off-line, telling visitors to his website. "Unlike all the romantic comedies and bad pop songs, you'll have to make up your own ending for this." However, his new girlfriend's employer soon started a new contest, offering people a date with the magazine's next "dream girl" from their intern pool.

Whether it is finding the girl of your dreams or deciding which car to purchase, people now depend on each other to help them, following simple rules that are not much different from the ones a flock of birds follows when it takes flight. Birds will flock where they are attracted and flee from where they are repulsed. This means that our mind-set must shift from one of simply getting our message in front of people to one of attracting them as they gather information from both you and each other.

Much of this flocking or fleeing behavior rests in the integrity of our own brands. People have told each other what they think since the dawn of time – except that they now influence a much bigger audience every time they rate you, blog about you, or flock to your website, just by following their own simple rules. So engaging them starts in the same place in which all marketing rests, with excellent products and services.

At the same time, the community has become your marketing department, in what is often a very literal sense. When they like you, they can create entire markets for you as they follow their own simple rules. And when they do not like you, the same simple rules can quickly blossom into the viral spread of bad service experiences, product exposes, and anti-corporate campaigns.

This is the point where my profession comes in. We know how people think, and we know what people want. We have a track record of making people aware of brands and building relationships with them. When you leverage this very creative and yet very quantitative art with the knowledge of how people behave, the future is limitless.

The age of reference fundamentally represents a shift in the balance of power between consumers and their brands. Once upon a time, brands had much of the upper hand: They held sway over things like pricing, consumer opinion, competitive information, and above all the brand message. Now that much of this information is just a mouse click away,

53

consumers control a lot more than just their own individual purchasing decisions. They ultimately control your brand identity.

Some people in business may find this shift a little disconcerting. I personally welcome it, for reasons that are both altruistic and selfish. On the altruistic side, a more open dialogue between brands and communities benefits the interests of everyone who purchases a product or service, and helps ensure better customer relationships. On the more selfish side, the power of co-creating a brand with your customers, together with the potential to leverage your marketing efforts to spread them across an entire community, is going to open up a new era for leading brands. As with good human relationships, I see much to look forward to from this new partnership of equals.

Why Speed Is the New Big

The beautiful island state of Hawaii has over one million residents. Together, they probably use about 40 million rolls of toilet paper ever year. But one of the greatest – and completely unintended – viral marketing feats in history made nearly every single roll disappear off the shelves of Hawaiian stores.

You see, Hawaii has many of its products shipped from the mainland of the United States. During the oil crisis of 1973, a rumor started that rising oil prices would mean fewer shipments of toilet paper. The result was a sudden, massive run on stores, cleaning out everyone's stock.

What happened here was the viral spread of information to a vast number of people in a very short period of time. The importance of this message was great enough, and the social connections on the islands were strong enough, that a small rumor spread contagiously until it was a great big buying frenzy.

Now let's move to the social networking era. When fans of the post-apocalyptic American television show *Jericho* learned that the series was being canceled by the CBS network, a fan from its online community made a unique suggestion: Send a bag of nuts to the network, inspired by the never-give-up epithet "Nuts!" uttered by one of the show's characters. CBS's studios were besieged with 20 *tons* of nuts from fans, and they soon relented and put the show back on the air.

And now let's go a step further, to the world of viral video. When you upload a video and get the right influencers talking about it, it is no longer unusual to have a swarm of millions flock to it. For example, a recent video of an American beauty pageant contestant flubbing a simple question has now been viewed over 30 million times, or once for every tenth man, woman, and child in the United States.

The Hawaiian toilet paper panic spread by word of mouth among people who knew each other. The *Jericho* protest spread among people who had an electronic connection with each other. But the spread of viral information throughout a digital community of people, many of whom *do not* know each other, usually takes place more quickly and involves many more people – often orders of magnitude more.

This is a game-changing trend for how we build and sustain brands. As marketing professionals, we have always measured our success in terms of *big:* how large a media buy, what size demographic, how many eyeballs we can deliver. Big still works very well in our business. But nowadays, the small group that spreads a message like wildfire can be even more valuable to you than capturing a percentage of a large herd. This means that speed, not size, has become the currency of the metaverse. Let's explore how this works, and what it means for you and your brand.

The anatomy of a blogstorm

56

We have grown accustomed to hearing about information exploding very quickly across cyberspace. For example, there have now been more than 70 million hits following the exploits of "lonelygirl15," an actress posing very convincingly as a teenage video blogger. So where do those million, or two million, or tens of millions of people that we keep hearing about come from?

They come from a phenomenon that is best explained by the difference between a web *page* and a web *log*, or blog. The genesis – and the genius – of swarm marketing exists in the difference between these two very similar yet very different things.

There are, at last count, more than 100 million blogs in cyberspace. More than 100,000 new ones are being added per day as I write this. So at first glance starting a blog might seem like planting a tree in the middle of a very deep forest, where no one will find it. But it isn't.

The difference lies in what we call a "feed," or the social network that surrounds each person's blog. While early web pages just sat there waiting for people to visit them, feeds turn blogs into living organisms. Most blogs and social networking sites can be set up so that whenever a blogger adds or changes something, it sends an update to everyone who has signed on to it. Technologies ranging from RSS feeds to "friend" links have now turned the web into a real, interconnected web.

This means that instead of a passive website that people individually watch like television, digital social networks live and breathe. And they disperse information *very* quickly. According to some studies, the average teenager has more than 40 online friends on social networking sites.[1] This is a small fraction of the nearly 500 real-life friends most of us make in a lifetime, yet it is an extraordinarily powerful number. What happens when

The traditional viral spread of information versus a blogstorm.

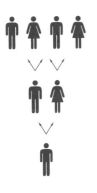

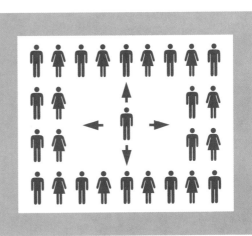

information goes to 40 people and they each pass it along to 40 more, and so forth? Do the math.

This is what we call a blogstorm, or a sudden eruption of swarm activity that spreads quickly across social networks. The mechanics of a blogstorm are another good example of where swarm marketing goes beyond viral marketing. The latter has its roots in epidemiology, the science of studying epidemics with real-world viruses: You sneeze, two people catch a cold, then they sneeze and infect four people, and so on.

Today's social networking environment turns epidemiology on its ear. When you "sneeze" on your blog or your social networking page, you may be infecting dozens or even hundreds of people – and if what they see engages them, it can quickly spread to thousands and millions with the click of a mouse.

The lurker effect

One of the keys to influencing a community is engaging the people who lurk beneath the surface.

Nearly five years ago, one of the largest-ever Internet fundraising efforts for an individual took place when Rocco Prestia, bass player for the legendary funk band Tower of Power, fell ill and needed a liver transplant.

Tower of Power has a dedicated fan community on the Internet, which at first glance seems like a small group of people: 200 to 300 active members, of whom 20 or 30 "core" fans posted regularly on their message board. In the summer of 2002, with no paid advertising whatsoever, this group launched a fundraising effort to pay for Rocco's medical bills and follow-up care that raised nearly US$200,000.

This effort started with one small seed: A longtime fan and web designer who had gotten to meet several band members took a call one day from TOP's lead singer, suggesting that he create a website for Rocco. Once the website went live, it was promoted with just one more small seed: an announcement on the message board.

From there, the seed spread to the thousands of people who "lurked" and quietly read this board without posting, from fans to music industry professionals. Within a few weeks it had spread far and wide to several other communities, including

- an online community of bass players who mounted a donation challenge;
- music and video companies that kicked in free merchandise, donations and promotions;
- nearly 60 fan "coordinators" in cities worldwide who manned local promotional campaigns;
- fellow musicians, including several big names in rock music, many of whom made large contributions and hosted benefit concerts;
- a large fan community in Japan that created its own website and raised almost 20 percent of the total.

By the time it concluded, the campaign raised enough money to help Prestia through his transplant and a subsequent major operation. Today he is healthy and back on tour, the lurkers have faded back into the background, and Tower of Power's small virtual community continues to hum along.

Of course, the operative word here is "engage." Engagement is the key to waking up the sleeping giant of a social network. The fundamental mind shift that our profession needs to make is not just from traditional media to interactive ones, or from a few channels to many. It is more a matter of changing the fundamental question we ask ourselves. Instead of asking "How do we attract people to our brand?" we need to ask "How do we get people to connect *with each other* about our brand?"

The speed and power of the social network lie in the answer to this new question. Take, for example, the website SimplyMarry.com, a matrimonial site in India run by Times Business Services Limited. You could simply advertise this site to families who will be planning weddings as well as to individuals who are looking for their soul mate. But how do you get people to tell each other to go there?

What Tribal DDB India did was tap into the interests of one of the most powerful forces in the wedding process: the mother-in-law. We set up a microsite to celebrate October 28 as Mother-in-Law Day, where both married and single people could post messages and video interviews expressing their feelings and opinions about their mothers-in-law, along with tips on how to get along with them. The idea was not just to bring out the love–hate relationship of people with their mothers-in-law, but to dwell on the good aspects of it for this one day. Simply put, SimplyMarry.com takes the responsibility to get its target group ready for the most delicate relationship of their lives.[2]

The result of this date-specific promotion was over 5,000 messages posted on the launch day alone – and a powerful viral force to get people to visit the site. Who *wouldn't* have their mother-in-law visit a tribute to her on the web? We accomplished these goals by giving people something of value – a tangible way to honor their families – while respecting the importance of the larger family in the wedding process.

This gets to the heart of what makes people flock quickly and virally to your brand: becoming a peer that attracts the community, which in turn creates a persistent brand identity. It is the same kind of symbiotic relationship we expect from our friendships. Increasingly, people are expecting this from their brand relationships as well.

The mechanics of a blogstorm underlie one of the most basic principles of swarm marketing: that digital communication has speeded up the way a swarm of consumers reacts and magnified its impact on your brand. Herd marketing is about how many – or what percentage – of people you can influence. Today marketing is about how you can touch points of leverage that influence thousands or millions of people quickly.

The Philips Bodygroom: creating a digital marketing outbreak

Social networks move very quickly when they share information with each other. But can you get them to talk about your product?

The key is that digital communities pass along things that interest or entertain them, in person or through the blogosphere. You probably understand people getting word around quickly about a hot music video or a breaking news story. But how do you get them talking about an electric shaver?

Men's grooming products are not traditionally a hot topic in the blogosphere. But when our client Philips Norelco created a new body trimmer designed for shaving below the neck, we saw an opportunity to get men to look at what was really important to most of them: attracting women. Moreover, we did it with a very edgy and funny campaign that created a network of men talking to each other about the ad *and* the product.

The centerpiece of this campaign was a video advertisement that you would most certainly never see on television. In it, a man in a bathrobe talks frankly about trimming body hair in a way that is rarely heard in polite company. For example, he starts out by saying things like, "Grooming

Pitching the benefits of the Philips Bodygroom in a viral video.

your back, chest, (bleep) and (bleep) demands a certain delicacy," while kiwi fruits, peaches, and carrots strategically appear on-screen in place of bleeped-out body parts.

62 After introducing the Philips Bodygroom, he wastes no time in getting down to the benefits: "With a well-groomed back, hair-free chest, and an extra optical inch on my (bleep), let's just say life has gotten pretty darn cozy." Soon afterward, a gushing voice mail from an enthusiastic female friend – with another bleeped-out carrot – makes the point even less subtly.

The rest of this ad – complete with a mock music video of the same man singing about how "on a scale of 1 to 10, my naked body was a 4.8" – ultimately directed people to the website shaveeverywhere.com, where people could watch the video, find out more about the product, and above all let their friends know.

From there, our marketing and PR campaigns took to the streets, both literally and virtually. We shared the product and the video with radio shock jock Howard Stern, who ran a provocative segment on how to look better to attract women. We spread the word to influential bloggers, put signs in bars, and ran banner ads on websites like Maxim and Men's Health. We even reached one place that guaranteed a male demographic, having talking ads in restroom urinals.

The results were nothing short of amazing. People spread our message throughout the digital universe almost instantly: Before long we were mentioned on over 2000 blogs and many major broadcast and print media outlets, ranging from *The New York Times* to CNBC, and had over a million website visits. And these visitors didn't just laugh at our edgy humor; they bought into our message. The Philips Bodygroom soon became the number-one personal care product on Amazon.com for eight weeks straight, becoming one of the most successful product launches in Amazon history, and quickly sold out in physical stores as well.

Ultimately, this new product category for Philips Norelco sold three times their projections in the first three months, and rose from nothing to gain a 70 percent share of the electric body-grooming category. Our own industry took notice as well, with a host of creative awards including the AdAge Digital Campaign of the Year and the Cannes Gold Cyber Lion award.

63

What made this campaign successful? First, we bet that an edgy, creative video that offered a clear benefit for men would get people talking to each other: Nearly 47 percent of the people we studied forwarded a link to the video to at least one of their friends. I would like to think that they were becoming brand evangelists, but am happy enough that forwarding racy humor to people led them to actually purchase the product.

Collateral print advertising for the Philips Bodygroom shaver.

We also did a very effective job of targeting our community. In the herd marketing era, we could never run a campaign like this in traditional print and broadcast media for a general audience to see. But by targeting young men in places they congregate, ranging from bars to blogs to shock-jocks (and the relatively censor-free world of satellite radio), we could reach this market with laser precision.

By reaching out to the swarm and engaging it, we launched a top-rated product for about the same amount of money that one US family might spend on a small starter house. Much of what we did leveraged the free and open access of the blogosphere and viral video, media that were an integral part of the lifestyle of the Bodygroom's target audience.

These kinds of results show what thinking like a community can do for your own products and services, which gets to the core of why I am so passionate about this new view of marketing. It gives your brand tremendous leverage that goes beyond throwing money at people to gain their attention. This, in turn, is how you evolve from attracting customers to creating sustainable brand communities.

Speed can work for or against you

What spreads more quickly: good news or bad news? Or to put it another way, would the swarm be more likely to spread your latest advertisement or their bad experiences with your product?

65

The speed and leverage of marketing today holds tremendous promise for you and your brand. It also holds tremendous peril. The nature of living in a digital community is that it can flock toward you quickly, but it can flock *at* you even quicker. Well-publicized recordings of people trying to get their wireless phone company to understand basic math or cancel their online service have become a form of entertainment as well as bad publicity. We grimace as one, but we also listen with rapt attention, in perhaps the same way that we are drawn to fictional soap operas.

niche where the audience feels 'this article was written just for me.' "[4] In a future with lots of different specialty channels, the lesson is that we not only can tailor our message to specific communities, but we must do so; Ketchum refers to it as "a public of one."

The footprints of the digital community have also become a fertile breeding ground for research; for example, academics are now using social networking sites to analyze everything from social patterns to crisis response, such as how people used Facebook to disseminate information about the Virginia Tech campus shootings of 2007.[5] From a marketing standpoint, we now have the data to understand consumer groups and target markets better than we ever have before.

This trend raises a host of privacy questions as well; for example, when someone posts their interests on a networking site, are they consenting to become part of someone else's data set? While there is no consensus at present on using individual data – and everyone agrees that posting a page on MySpace is not an invitation to get unwanted spam from marketers – there is now clearly a gold mine of aggregate data that can tell us what people want and how best to give it to them.

It also changes the way we measure things. The metrics for following effective online marketing have evolved considerably these days, growing from measuring clicks to looking at broader measures of brand interaction. This suggests a move from return on investment to "return on involvement," where we are involving a client in an experience and creating brand demand. In this view, the only way to avoid getting skipped is to be entertaining and magnetic enough to attract people.

I frankly feel that we have a lot more work to do in the area of measuring our effectiveness with digital communities. First, what most people consider to be "online metrics" are basically herd marketing metrics in cyberspace. Far be it from me to bash things like clickthrough rates, blog hits, or podcast subscribers – they are important measures of one kind of influence. But in my mind there is little difference between, say, what percentage of people click an online banner ad and how many people watch a television ad. You are still measuring what percentage of eyeballs respond to a promotional message.

Second, effective community-level engagement involves behaviors that go far beyond the point of contact. You want people to say good things about you and other people to see these good things as they flock to wherever they go. Ideally, you want people to take ownership and spread your message far beyond your own advertising. To me, measures of influence are as important with the swarm as measures of response.

Third and perhaps most important, we are too often asking the question "how many" or "what percentage" when the real question should be "how fast." The rate at which a message spreads through a social network is an important measure of attraction, and the ability to spread these messages consistently speaks to the relationship between the community and your brand. It is in this third area where we perhaps have the most work ahead of us.

All of these issues point toward a more fundamental shift, from point of purchase efforts to community-building ones. We all want people to buy our products and services, and advertising – whether it is on the side of a bus or at the top of a blog – can be very effective in making that happen. But the era of digital connectivity is moving us beyond the concept of selling things over and over and toward building communities that flock toward us, multiply quickly, and make our brands part of the rhythm of their lives.

69

Breaking down the voice of the consumer

In a digital era, millions of conversations are taking place every day between consumers and their brands. They are asking us for information, giving us feedback, and seeking our service. Increasingly, they are also becoming part of the co-creation process that helps us develop our products and services.

So how do you listen to what consumers are telling you, particularly as the amount of information coming at us continues to explode? Increasingly, people are looking toward formal analytics as well as human interaction to turn the collective voice of the swarm into actionable advice.

For example, a recent white paper report "How Consumer Conversation Will Transform Business" from PricewaterhouseCoopers proposes monitoring relative movements in areas such as the number of times a subject is mentioned, positive or negative tone, coverage in terms of number of sources, and how authoritative or influential these sources are.

While analytics still revolve around text-based messages such as e-mails or blog entries, tools for extracting meaning and emotions from audio and video touch points are increasingly being talked about as well. But we are still a long way from making these tools part of our routine: According to this report, surveys showed that over 60 percent of respondents saw having the right systems to analyze data, and the right people to interpret it, as a challenge.

We will probably never fully automate our relationship with consumers, nor should we – but mining its collective intelligence and using it to benefit them are likely to become key parts of how market leaders engage the community.

(*Source*: "How Consumer Conversations Will Transform Business," PricewaterhouseCoopers white paper series, Jan. 2008.)

From size to speed: a world where everything is digital

They say that power corrupts, and perhaps the same thing is true for speed in the digital era.

Every technological revolution is like this. Once we started driving cars, it became very hard to get back on a horse. When people began to get washing machines, they stopped beating their wet clothes with a stick to clean them. And for those of you who have a BlackBerry in your pocket and a laptop on your desk, when was the last time you pulled out a pen and wrote someone a letter?

The speed and urgency of the digital era are having the same effect on us. When it comes to hearing your message, consumers have less patience for what they don't want or need. Conversely, when they want something, they want it now. Today's consumers demand things in real time, whether it is information, services, or products.

This is why the distinction between "online marketing" and all marketing is fading away. Moreover, the urgency and immediacy of online marketing are becoming influences that now color all marketing. Ultimately, these trends will lead us toward a world where we know more about our clients than ever before, and where we use this knowledge to help people flock toward us. Our profession once viewed success as launching an advertisement and attracting a very dim percentage of the eyeballs that saw it. From here, we need to start thinking about building customer communities who seek us out.

In the future, we have much to learn from the way a juicy story or viral video erupts through its audience, or how people make their brand choices in a social network. The answers to questions like these will involve things like psychology and even biology as well as marketing. In time, this knowledge will evolve to become a consistent philosophy of engaging both communities and the individuals within them, and before long we will simply be calling it "marketing." I personally feel that our craft is on the verge of becoming much more powerful and effective – and in the process it is going to become a lot more fun.

The First Law of Engaging a Community: Conviction

What's in a name?

I spent a great deal of my career helping organizations answer that question, as the CEO of global branding consultancy Interbrand a few years ago. Our firm started out in the 1970s creating names and packaging for companies, and then creating brands, and more recently, helping clients understand and optimize the value of these brands.

Today it is clear that brands have real, tangible worth. If you create the most delicious cherry-flavored cola drink in the world, marketing it as Wild Cherry Pepsi will give it a market value far above and beyond selling the same beverage as a generic product. In the same way, we look for great guest experiences from Marriott, expect FedEx to get our packages delivered on time, and trust products from the Clorox Company to get our laundry clean and fresh.

The value of a brand is perhaps the single most important asset of a company. Years ago, I helped author an annual ranking of the world's most valuable brands together with *BusinessWeek* magazine, and we found that the impact of a brand on incremental revenues and projected future earnings often far exceeds other factors. For example, the top-five global brands alone have a combined brand value of nearly a quarter of a trillion dollars, and it is not unusual for such top-ranked brands to have values that are several times their annual revenues.[1]

So what is a brand, really? Is it a good name? Many companies like ExxonMobil or eBay have names that have nothing to do with their business. Or how about great products and services? They are very important, but some of our most cherished brands have survived stumbles ranging from New Coke to the collapse of IBM's mainframe computer market. And what about size and market share? Just ask anyone who used to work for Enron, once the seventh-biggest company in the United States.

To me, the essence of a brand is that it stands for something in the mind of your business: something fundamental that you believe about yourself and that the public believes as well. I call this trait *conviction*.

Take Harley-Davidson, the great American motorcycle manufacturer. Harley-Davidson is not only considered the epitome of the classic American motorcycle: it is also known around the world as a symbol of independence and freedom. Its identity – and its brand community – can perhaps best be summed up by the "creed" found on its website. Written in the form of a prayer, it speaks of "bucking a system that is built to smash individuals like bugs on a windshield" and champions "motorcycle rallies that last a week."[2]

This creed is more than just advertising copy. It sums up what leads many people around the world to own and ride Harleys, and it sums up how the brand sees itself. Examples like these sit at the core of showing conviction in a marketplace.

Behind every brand there is a great idea. All brands start in the same place, with the personal vision and conviction of the marketers behind them. To me, brands are like people, and the best ones have always stood for something. They are authentic, consistent, and true to themselves, and people follow them.

Conviction and digital communities

Everything I have just said could be taken straight out of a Branding 101 textbook. It is fundamental to my profession. So what does this have to do with influencing a digital community?

Here is the connection. Look at the top 100 websites in the United States, as one example, and see where people are flocking:

- First, you will find the tools of digital community itself: search engines like Google and Yahoo!, social networking sites like MySpace and Facebook, and agent-maintained information sources like Wikipedia and BizRate.com.
- Next, you will find websites for many brands that were well established outside of cyberspace: Target, Best Buy, Wal-Mart, Sears, Dell.
- Finally, you will find things that attract the community members, including news, financial information, and entertainment sites.

When you move from there to the global top 100, you will see that similar tools in other countries form the bulk of this list, such as China's Baidu.com search engine. It is here on this global stage, within a digitally connected swarm, that the value of your brand identity – in other words, your conviction about your products and services – comes into sharper focus than ever.

75

Go to a shopping mall in the United States and you may see a Sears and a J.C. Penney store down the hall from each other. Land at a major US airport and you are likely to see Hertz, Avis, and Alamo rental car counters. Go shopping for groceries in Europe and you will find Metro, Carrefour, and others. Big markets in the herd economy tend to have a wide range of competitors.

Digital communities are different. When you fly along with them, you will find they often flock quickly to places they like and stay there.

Amazon.com doesn't just sell more books than its nearest competitor's website, they sell a *lot* more. The Apple iPod, which didn't exist at the beginning of new millennium, now represents close to three-quarters of the market for digital music players.[3] And for every person who does a search on Altavista.com, one of the first Internet search engines, nearly 70 do so on Google.[4]

This doesn't mean that digital connectivity always leads to monopolies. For example, Yahoo!, with less than 20 percent of the search engine market share, is still a big company with a market value in the tens of billions of US dollars. More important, as we will see later, the era of the swarm opens up an endless stream of niche markets. But the three brands here – Amazon.com, Apple's iPod, and Google – all serve as examples of a strong brand identity being the scent that attracts the crowd.

All of these brands stand for something. If you ask a random sample of people what they stand for, you will get very similar answers: the biggest online marketplace on Earth, the simplest and most widely accepted music player, and an easy, fast, and accurate search engine. Let's look at the convictions behind these three brands in a little more detail.

Amazon.com

Amazon.com can be seen as an online bazaar for everyone else's products, from DVDs to dishwashers. Originally an online bookstore when it began life in the mid-1990s, it has become one of the biggest destinations on the Internet in countries around the world. But it is just a storefront in a virtual world with many storefronts. So why do people shop at Amazon.com, even when there are numerous websites that might undercut the price of an item, or even compare Amazon prices with lots of other vendors?

The answer is that Amazon has a brand identity. When it began life, it had a slogan of "Earth's biggest bookstore." Today, as it has expanded to become a global marketplace of everything from toothpaste to furniture, its current slogan is "...and you're done." In both cases, it successfully created a mindshare for one-stop shopping on the Internet.

As a web-based venture from day one, Amazon.com is also an example of attracting people around a brand image. Many people who visit Amazon aren't buying anything: They are browsing products, reading and making comments, and contributing to a collective intelligence – and this stickiness, in turn, brings them back when they are ready to buy.

Ironically, Amazon maintains this brand identity without many of the trappings of most companies its size. It has no bricks-and-mortar presence whatsoever. It does almost no advertising in traditional media. It even maintains exceptionally high customer-satisfaction ratings despite its well-publicized refusal to publish its toll-free telephone number for customer service.

This brand image keeps its customers loyal despite a virtual world with hundreds or thousands of other purchasing options. In keeping this conviction of building a virtual community where people could buy (and later sell) practically anything – and more important, talk to each other about it – Amazon rose far above many bricks-and-mortar entrants to its online niche, *and* above the ability to easily search online for cheaper prices elsewhere. That image, and not just its prices on the latest books or DVDs, is what drives people toward it.

Apple's iPod

Apple was not the first company to create a personal music player that fits in your pocket. Nor was it the first to market a personal media player that evolved to have movies, games, and other features. But the sleek, elegant design and plug-and-play ease of use of its iPod family did not just capture people's attention: It was a rebirth for Apple, the company whose "think differently" mantra previously spoke to a niche market in the computer industry.

The success of the iPod certainly was not for lack of competition. Other manufacturers of MP3 players did everything but stand on their heads to offer more features, ranging from recording capabilities to built-in radio tuners. Several even took aim at the core economic model behind the iPod: Instead of purchasing music by the track from Apple's iTunes service, many of these players could be loaded up with as many songs as you wanted from inexpensive subscription services.

So why does the iPod continue to crush everyone in terms of market share? It started with a critical moment of truth as the market first opened up: Apple products are known for their ease of use and human ergonomics, and iPod was no exception. While some early competitors produced devices with a rat's nest of drivers and configuration software that only a geek could love, iPods basically plugged in and worked. And even if you saw one for the first time on a desert island, you could use it intuitively to play music and watch videos. Today these devices are part of a family that ranges from tiny music players the size of your thumb to the wireless connectivity of the iPhone.

In developing the iPod, Apple built a swarm market around people who embody its greatest brand attribute – innovation. By giving these people permission to experiment and even fail, the company has once again come to represent leading-edge technology solutions that are part of day-to-day life. Today Apple is embedded tangibly and emotionally in its customers' habits and practices. In the process, they have created a brand community of epic proportions.

Google

Search engines are our window onto the Internet. They are our guide to an online world that is growing faster than we can keep up with it.

Moreover, they have become the enabling tool for the behavior of digital communities.

There are literally hundreds of search engines. They range from sites with human guides, like ChaCha.com, to sites that regularly give away million-dollar prizes like iWon.com. So why do nearly two out of every three searches take place on Google nowadays? For that matter, why (despite the wishes of Google's legal team) has its name become a commonly used verb?

The answer is that they did something that attracted the crowd and kept them there. Or, more accurately, two crowds. One flocked to its ease of use and the relevancy of its searches, the other to an open-source architecture that led Google searches to be embedded in everything from your browser to Aunt Mabel's recipe site. In both cases, they started building a brand community.

Today Google does many "sticky" things to keep attracting people. It gives you free e-mail, hosts your videos, manages online communities, prints maps, and lets you read books online. More recently, as the world has become more wireless, it introduced a service where you can request via text message that Google send directions or restaurant recommendations to your phone. It even offers free telephone directory assistance to look up phone numbers without ever getting near a computer.

79

Google does not advertise on television. There is no Google blimp or Google Stadium (at least yet). And it was far from the first company to produce a search engine in the heady days of the 1990s dot-com boom. But a few simple rules, combined with a lot of free goodies that attract the masses, have created one of the strongest brand identities in the world.

The sense of conviction found in companies like these influences how you market to the herd, but has an even greater influence on how you market at a community level. In particular, it underscores the need to stand for something in the eyes of the swarm.

All three of these brands have a strong sense of who they are: a conviction that, in turn, influences both their business strategy and their marketing. In the process, they have not only built competitive businesses, but have also experienced the breathtaking growth of market share – and mindshare – that comes with influencing today's digital community. They have become part of their collective intelligence, and will likely remain there until someone with more conviction dislodges them.

The process that happens when people say, "What's on your iPod?" or "Google me," without even asking about your brand preferences, is where the nexus of a strong brand image and a digital community of customers lies. This is the promise, and the urgency, of knowing yourself and your niche in the new marketplace.

Linking your brand image to the community

Let's look at a case study of how we reengineered a brand image to attract a community. Volkswagen began life as the car for everyman: Its name literally translates to "the people's car." From its postwar roots producing inexpensive Beetles for the mass market to its current position as the fourth-largest car producer in the world, it had been long seen as the practical alternative for the mass market of car buyers.

DDB faced a challenge with today's Volkswagen: how to reestablish its image in Germany as "the people's car," in a world that now had many entry-level vehicles – and in a world where Volkswagen itself had expanded to make everything from sports cars to large luxury sedans.

Our answer came in the form of Horst Schlämmer: a coarse, unshaven German everyman in a rumpled grey trenchcoat, played by popular comedian Hape Kerkeling. Horst had a problem common to many men: He had trouble meeting women, and realized he needed a driver's license to catch a "bunny." We started a video blog of Horst's exploits taking driving lessons, sitting in classes, and finally shopping for cars, while

German everyman and Volkswagen spokesperson Horst Schlämmer learning to drive.

having misadventures ranging from getting stuck in an imported microcar to ramming a BMW during a test drive.

This funny story spread like wildfire: Soon it was the number two blog in all of Germany, as well as the number one podcast, and his exploits were followed closely by the German print and broadcast media. People could interact with Horst on his blog and spread his videos throughout cyberspace on sites like YouTube. It wasn't until well after people got hooked on the story that they realized that Volkswagen was sponsoring it, and by the time Horst purchased his own shiny, comfortable VW he had a massive following.

This successful campaign engaged people with a minimum of traditional advertising. But it made an even more important point: reinforcing the conviction behind Volkswagen's brand image. You see, the people who laughed at Horst Schlämmer's videos learned and remembered what Volkswagen's core conviction is: making practical cars for everyday people.

While Horst was very funny, there was a serious point behind the promotion. In recent years, Volkswagen has evolved into a product line that ranges from practical subcompacts to a super luxury flagship sedan costing over US$60,000. What made VW different from a Mercedes-Benz that was moving down-market, a BMW that was resurrecting economy cars like the Mini, or any of a number of luxury car brands that competed with its flagship Phaeton?

What ultimately made Volkswagen different was its conviction about what it is: a global car company that emphasizes brains over brawn and practicality over ego. Not the largest carmaker in the world, nor the highest-performance one, but the one that most closely meets the needs of everyman: the people's car. In our relationship with Volkswagen we have learned the importance of how a company's branding and products go hand in hand. Today, in an era of digital connectivity, we have also learned how your image, in and of itself, can attract a brand community.

Creating "brand bigotry"

The story of Volkswagen makes a much larger point about sharing your conviction with the swarm. Did you notice that this campaign does not focus on the car itself?

There is no talk of horsepower, safety features, navigation systems, or anything else that most people would think should be part of selling an automobile. Instead, the goal is simply to share Volkswagen's conviction with people, and hopefully help people internalize it as part of their *own* values. After that, the "horsepower" talk can take place between people and their individual dealers.

You can think of this as "brand bigotry," a term that *Fast Company* columnist Rob Walker coined to describe people who see brands as an extension of their personal values.[5] I like to think of it as a case where the right brand values change the simple rules that agents of a digital community follow. The person who says "I always wear Levis" or "My computer is always a Dell" is talking about his or her own self and not just your brand.

When people view brands as part of their identity, it can transcend seemingly rational factors such as price, features, or even the product itself. It is an emotional connection between individuals and your brand. When someone tells you that he rides a Harley, it doesn't matter what model it is or how many cc's the engine has: That person is telling you that he is a free spirit, and that this brand is part of who he is.

So how do you create this kind of "brand bigotry"? It starts with the basics: You must have a strong, creditable brand identity to leverage social networks, and you must successfully target points of influence within these networks. From there, the execution is just as important: delivering on your brand promise, having superior products and services, delivering unique customer experiences, and committing to a process of continuous innovation.

These are all good things. In fact, they are critically important things. But I feel that creating an emotional connection with your brand goes a step further. To get people to carry your brand around in their hearts and minds, *you* have to stand for something, and that "something" needs to resonate with the community. Whether it is the exclusivity of Chanel or the comfortable familiarity of Quaker oatmeal, one of the most important factors in engaging this community is making the leap from consumers' minds to their hearts.

83

Toyota Corolla versus Chevrolet Nova: An example of brand bigotry

In the 1980s Toyota and General Motors started a joint venture in the United States, producing cars for each other in the same plant. Their first product, released in the 1985 model year, reintroduced GM's longstanding Chevrolet Nova brand as a rebadged version of the popular Toyota Corolla.

Despite the fact that these cars were nearly identical – and despite appeals to "buy American" – the Corolla far outsold the Nova. Creating a new brand of Geo for Chevrolet joint-venture cars did not help the situation: By the late 1990s Toyota Corollas were outselling the similar Geo Prizm by a margin of nearly three to one, despite now being built in the same factory, and the Prizm often required rebates to move inventory. Even after a return to the Chevrolet nameplate in the late 1990s, the value of a 2002 Prizm was nearly US$2,000 less than its Toyota cousin, according to 2006 NADA figures.

More than two decades since the start of this joint venture, its latest car continues this trend: As of mid-year sales figures in 2007, retail sales of the Toyota Matrix exceeded those of the similar Pontiac Vibe by more than fifty percent, while a two-year-old Matrix commands a trade in value roughly US$500 greater than a similarly-equipped Vibe.

(*Sources*: Edmunds.com, NUMMI.com, fleet-central.com, NADA. com.)

Why would someone pay a premium for one brand of car versus another, even though it is common knowledge that they are identical cars? Here is where the conviction of your brand's message influences the direction the masses follow. Each individual makes his or her buying decisions based on simple rules that exist at several levels of the process:

- One level of this process operates on a purely factual level: namely, what is the history of this person and others in the community with this brand?

- Next, there is a perceptional level: What kind of brand does someone want to be seen with or associated with by others?
- Finally, there is a meta-level that involves community-level awareness and not just brand awareness: Regardless of how someone feels about affiliating with a particular brand, his or her awareness of the community's perception of these brands influences their expectations for things like resale value.

This is where the heart of brand conviction and engaging a community exists. In a herd, it is all about you. You are fed marketing messages and react to them – or not. In a swarm community, we are all exquisitely aware of what everyone *else* is thinking and feeling, which often compels us to fly in formation with the others. This means that your message is no longer just about a benefit for a buyer: Now, more than ever, it must become a badge of identification for a social group that flocks together.

Putting conviction into action: What principles create global brands?[6]

Having brand conviction is one of those principles that everyone understands, at least in hindsight. This is even more critical today in an era of social networks where members are linked electronically and not geographically.

There are a number of traits that make a successful brand. Some of these traits include a compelling idea, an engaging brand message, and a great product. For example, at FedEx doing things accurately and on time matter above everything, while Ritz-Carlton employees share a fanaticism about their guest experiences. This "internal" branding then, in turn, drives the message behind your external brand.

From there, perhaps the biggest change is that our message needs to be a global one and not just a personal one – one that reaches in and touches the hearts of the members of a community that is no longer bounded by geography. There are a consistent set of principles shared by successful brands as they go global: recognition, consistency, emotion, uniqueness, and adaptability. Here is how they apply to your brand:

Recognition

Well-performing brands enjoy strong awareness among consumers and opinion leaders. They create a uniform brand image in most people, even when they are not the brand's customers. Think BMW. Car aficionados, reviewers, and loyal customers laud it with equal enthusiasm. It has come to symbolize performance in engineering and design while signifying that the owner has "arrived" on a personal and professional level. This type of recognition binds perception and reality, enabling brands to rapidly establish credibility in new markets.

Consistency

Leading brands achieve a high degree of consistency in visual, verbal, sonic, and tactile identity, in their neighborhood and around the world. They deliver a consistent customer experience that is often supported by an integrated global marketing effort. McDonald's is an example of a brand that has simplified its core message and offer, and communicates a consistent shared message worldwide. This is not to say that other firms do not ever modify their approaches for regional relevance, but it does mean that any member of the McDonald's swarm knows what to expect from the brand.

Emotion

We talked earlier about creating an emotional connection between people and your brand, but to me this should go a step further. A brand is not a brand unless it fundamentally competes in the emotional dimension.

It must symbolize a promise that people believe can be delivered and one they desire to be part of.

Through emotion, brands can attract people by tapping into human values and aspirations that cut across cultural differences. Nike has appealed to the athlete in all, regardless of true physical ability, allowing for a focused yet mass-market offer. This has elevated the discussion beyond tangible aspects of the shoe or apparel to what the customer feels when wearing and performing in Nike gear.

Uniqueness

Great brands represent great ideas. These brands express a unique position to all internal and external audiences. They effectively use all elements in the communications mix to position themselves within their markets. The swarm has no doubt about what Facebook, Apple, or Southwest Airlines stands for, and their marketing efforts reinforce this message.

Adaptability

Global brands must respect local needs, wants, and tastes. These brands adapt to the local marketplace while fulfilling a global mission. For example, HSBC – true to its roots as the British-based Hong Kong and Shanghai Banking Corporation – has invested in that very message by conveying its excellence in financial services with its deep knowledge of local custom and practice. In essence, it is communicating a "glocal" advantage.

87

Is there such a thing as "glocal"?

Successful global brands often take a globally appealing brand message, such as the "premium" and "elite" identity of fashion leader Chanel, and apply it in local circumstances. This is achieved by translating the message in a locally relevant way; for example, in 2004 the company produced a three-minute film featuring Nicole Kidman to promote its Chanel No. 5 fragrance in the English-speaking market, investing a budget comparable to that of many full-length films.

If the brand has more than one distinguishing feature, the message can be tailored to the local audience. For example, Mercedes plays up their prestigious brand positioning in the Chinese market while it concentrates on its reputation for quality in Germany.

This "glocal" quality springs from giving local managers the power to interpret and express the message. This does not mean that global brands must be nationless, as long as their core characteristics have international appeal; in fact, country of origin can easily form a core brand identity that is easily recognizable around the world. For example, McDonald's is associated with America but its brand identity of good value, quick-service food resonates globally. The goal is to communicate in many languages but with one voice.

If you could sum these all up in one neat package, it would be that you have to live the conviction of your brand, particularly if you want other people to live it. This process starts at the top of an organization, ideally with a CEO who continually articulates your brand philosophy and its view of the world, and continues through to every touch point between your business and its brand community. If there is one common denominator among brands that attract swarms, it is a corporate culture that puts its brand at the heart of everything it does, and *in* the hearts of consumers who follow it.

This does not imply that your message is everything, as much as people in my business wish it were so. You need to sweat the details in everything else that creates memorable brand experiences, including superior products, processes, and people, being customer-centric, having the right ethical practices, and keeping a continual focus on creativity and innovation.

At the same time, look carefully at the things you buy – and the brands you surround yourself with. Are they just cold, rational purchasing decisions based on specifications, or do you *feel* something about these brands? This is where the digital communities will be leading your brand in the future. In the end, it starts and ends with the conviction of your message.

6

The Second Law of Engaging a Community: Collaboration

How would you characterize your own social life? In fact, how would you compare the community of people you know to the one your parents know – or your children?

The drive to form communities is as old as civilization. For many centuries, we shared information and fellowship in places like the English pub, the American town square, and the Chinese teahouse. Back then, we socialized in groups. But fast-forward to a twentieth century with electricity, suburbia, and mass media, and society had slowly turned into a herd. A typical situation comedy from the 1960s showed families cocooned in their homes, or perhaps playing canasta with their next-door neighbors. Above all, we gathered around the television set instead of seeking entertainment and intellectual stimulation in each other.

This was the point in time when modern herd marketing took shape. Our industry has its roots in a post–World War II generation of mass media, where people gathered around these media channels passively waiting to be told what to do and buy. When DDB began life in 1949 as Doyle Dane Bernbach, we thrived and flourished in this world, even as our founders set us apart by saying, "Let's stop talking at people and let's start conversations that lead to action."

Today, what we said more than a half century ago is now happening: We are returning to a world where conversations lead to action, this time on a global scale and much faster. Newer generations in particular are flocking to places like social networking sites and other virtual gathering places; in Europe, for example, the heaviest 20 percent of users spend nearly one out of every five waking hours there. Our digital "pub" has become bigger, more connected, and more present in our lives than ever before.

We have once again become a collaborative community, and its members now span the globe. The People 2.0 generation isn't sitting in front of a single television channel waiting to see your ad. They are interacting with each other through an ever-increasing network of channels. Above all, they are touching the same points of influence and reacting as a group.

This means that your brand also has to collaborate with a community, so that it flocks toward you. Once upon a time, not that long ago, people would create products and services and then talk with people like me to create advertising for them. Today your customers themselves want to have a say in what you do and how you can do it better.

Look closely at the new generation of market leaders and you will see product marketing being replaced by interactive brand communities. Customers now tell Dell what the next system will be on its production line. When McDonald's builds a new restaurant, feedback from the community is often part of its architecture. And at an even deeper level, companies like Nike are bringing virtual communities of runners together in the real world.

Marketing can no longer be a separate function, nor can it remain a one-way form of communication. Today it must become part of the conversation that surrounds your products, your services, and your marketing – and marketing itself must become a collaborative process that draws from this collective intelligence. Herds only require a one-way relationship, but communities require a conversation.

This sense of collaboration between you and the community can exist at several levels. At one level, you may track and listen to what its collective intelligence tells you. At another level, it may become a central part of your business model, where customers have a direct say in what you do. At still another level, you may become an agent for linking these communities together. Finally, your internal stakeholders can become a more important part of this dialogue than you thought.

Come with me on a walk through each of these levels and see what they are going to mean for brands and their businesses – and why these brands *must* collaborate with communities of consumers in the future.

Listening to the voice of the crowd: bloodless coups versus partnerships

Who was most responsible for creating downloadable music on the Internet? Was it Apple's iTunes? The first or second generations of Napster? The recording industry?

Actually, it was none of the above. *You* were responsible for digital music. As soon as technology allowed music to be stored electronically, you and the rest of the swarm sprang into action. Years before anyone ever held an iPod in his or her hand, people started sharing digital music files, whether recording companies liked it or not. You and your peers soon started linking your music collections with those of people you had never met face-to-face, and nothing could stop you.

When file-sharing networks for digital music first started to appear in the late 1990s, we lived in a world where record companies controlled the business model for music. You had to buy entire albums of songs, whether you liked every song or not. The distribution of music was limited to a few retailers. This album-and-record-store model formed the basis of the music industry for nearly a century, from the economics of making a record to the logistics of distributing a successful hit.

That's where you came in. All of the steps that led to today's digital music environment – legal downloads, music by the track, licensing agreements with major record labels, MP3 players, and software like iTunes – came in response to pressure from the collective marketplace. You, in the plural sense of the world, decided how music should be sold, and all the stakeholders in the music industry ultimately had to follow you. Today's legal music downloading environment resulted from a popular democratic uprising as much as it did a conceived business model. You staged a bloodless coup and won.

Corporate strategy expert C. K. Prahalad refers to this process as "co-creation," where a swarm of consumers plays a key partnership role with businesses in forging the future of products. He describes the path from illegal downloading to today's online music business as a shift from a company-centric system to a consumer-centric one.[1] I would take it a step further, and say that it is an example of what can happen to any business when customers are linked to form a single and powerful digital voice.

Of course, digital music is an example of co-creation that took place at the point of a gun or, more accurately, a mouse click. Perhaps a more benevolent example is how e-commerce sites have evolved to become collaborative communities.

We've come to take for granted that when we shop online, we can actively rate merchandise, participate in forum discussions, and even respond to and rate each other's comments. On Amazon.com, for example, customers can now post videos and "wikis" (editable linked content) about products, and share tips and support information. Product creators can be part of this dialogue as well – for example, it is not unusual for a major recording artist to post a direct response to an online comment, as well as talking to their fans by posting their own blogs, videos, and content. As people want more information and more dialogue when they buy things, the line between online shopping and social networking gets blurrier.

Most bricks and mortar stores would never let you post a sign saying that a product stinks or suggesting another one. Nor could you come into these stores with a problem and ask the other customers to help you fix it. Nor could you have a dialogue with the people who created the products themselves. But in virtual stores like Amazon.com, iTunes, and eBay, we now take all of this for granted. E-commerce sites have fundamentally changed the way we buy and interact with products because they leverage the voice of the crowd.

This is why people who buy products and services are now looking less like individuals and more like a community. Even traditional herd marketing itself is changing under the weight of this trend; for example, Google recently did a pilot project that uses aggregated data from set-top boxes to deliver custom television ads to specific groups, using the same kind of auction model they use for their online advertising. We may not be far from a day when individual communities tell us what kinds of advertising they want to see in the mass media.

What does this mean for you and your business? In my view, it means that the way we build brands and markets today is integrally tied into listening to your customers. If they are telling you that they want digital music, or a new product, or a connection with other consumers, they will make it happen. This means that if you want to stick with the old way of making things and advertising them to the herd, you risk being run over by businesses that create brand communities. That is why, in a very real sense, attracting the masses now starts with listening to them.

Listening deeper: CRM and the digital community

When a waiter swipes your credit card at a restaurant, you call your phone company for service, or you buy a new product someone advertised, do you realize that you just became part of a vast ocean of data? The electronic information most of us leave behind as we live our lives tells us things like,

- how many people eat steak on Fridays at T.G.I. Friday's;
- the single most profitable thing for your phone company to improve;
- how effective a new advertising campaign is for a specific product.

We marketing professionals have a name for this information. Or, more accurately, three initials: C-R-M. Short for Customer Relationship Management, CRM involves gathering data from all of the touch points between you and the businesses you use and analyzing it for trends. It has turned the concept of a digital community into a living, breathing organism that leaves big, fat footprints behind wherever it goes.

CRM allows businesses to get into your heads. (In some cases literally: According to a recent *Wall Street Journal* article, some organizations now read the brain waves of volunteers to see how they react during political debates.[2]) The data that come from these individuals then become part of a unified whole we can see and touch.

CRM can be a good thing: It can help companies learn what you want and do a better job of giving it to you. We can tell when you prefer later shopping hours or bigger portions of clam chowder. And it helps us create big ideas like iPhones or 24-hour service. It lets our customers speak to us, if we listen to it.

It can also be a bad thing. CRM can lead companies to order people to spend no more than 5.2 minutes with you – or focus on just their most profitable clients and ignore the long tail of everyday customers who govern their brand's reputation. Too much of today's CRM is actually customer monologue management, a one-way conversation where customers speak and no one responds, except perhaps at some disengaged strategic level.

Even worse, CRM can tempt companies to go beyond the bounds of good sense and privacy, as social networking giant Facebook recently learned the hard way: it aborted a plan to broadcast selected web activities of its members without first asking permission.[3] I believe that the growth of digital communities like Facebook is what has given rise to true, communicative social networks, but unless we are careful we can set into motion the community's instinctual sense to flock or flee, and risk becoming a predator instead of a protector.

Digital communities are changing the way we look at CRM. They will help us get back to doing CRM, in the true meaning of the word relationship: an ongoing, interactive dialogue between your brand and your customers. Yet the same tools, used from a different point of view, can help build the kind of collaborative relationships that lead people to flock toward you.

Take the LEGO Group of Denmark. Their tiny interlocking toy bricks, produced at the rate of over two billion per year, can build everything from simple play structures to complex electromechanical robots and massive works of art. Their LEGO® Creator website encourages customers to submit their own models for possible selection by LEGO as new kits.[4] Customers themselves vote on the best designs, and their creators are paid a generous five percent royalty from sales.

This is a classic example of emergence. LEGO has no idea as to what its next product kit will look like: The swarm decides. You can extend this to every other aspect of digital community behavior. No one ever imagined Amazon.com and eBay before the emergence of the Internet, certainly not the traditional bookstore and auction industries, yet without them we wouldn't have a viral network of buyers and sellers creating emerging patterns of what we buy and sell online. When you

97

turn the reins over to your customers, things that you never anticipated happen.

Of course, LEGO toys themselves are a model of emergence. Founder Ole Kirk Christiansen probably never envisioned today's massive LEGO brick structures when he created the first ones in the 1940s. These bricks, with tolerances so strict that bricks from 40 years ago will still fit models today, serve as the agents. Unleashing a flock of consumers on them has led to things like art festivals, amusement parks in Europe and the United States, and even a hit music video totally animated with LEGO bricks.[5]

Model of London's Trafalgar Square constructed of LEGO® bricks, as seen in LEGOland Windsor (UK).

Source © 2003 Kaihsu Tai. Permission granted under Wikimedia Commons.

Digital communities represent a brand new day for CRM. They will transform it from mountains of data we sift through to points of leverage influencing an entire population. We see it when many of Facebook's 50 million users are already relaying product or brand picks to friends. We see it when LEGO, whose name itself translates to the Latin term for

"I collect; I gather; I learn," embraces its customers to serve as its design team. More important, CRM now truly has the potential to become the link between your brand and collaborative customer relationships.

Moving the community into your business model

Have you ever said that the customer comes first in your business?

Every business says that it is close to its customers. But the reality is that most of them aren't. Customers still do not get to decide what is on the menu at most restaurants, they cannot order their next car in bright pink, and no one asked most of them what New York's new Yankee Stadium or Shanghai's Jin Mao Tower should look like. The vast majority of us are still wedded to the "push" model of marketing, where we decide what we are going to do, we do market research to see how many people might purchase it, and then we use advertising and promotion to convince these people to do so.

There are still very few firms who put customers at the heart of their business model, and truly let them decide what we are going to do and how we are going to do it. It is a huge and scary leap from suggestion boxes and focus groups to putting customers in the driver's seat at a real, operational level. Yet many firms who do exactly that are seeing results and teaching us lessons that are nothing short of revolutionary:

Take Dell. It started selling computers in a dorm room in the 1980s, using the revolutionary idea of selling systems to customer specifications instead of creating them in advance. Within a year, this dorm room business was grossing over US$70 million per year, and today this exact same model – building nearly every computer to customer specifications – remains the foundation of what is now one of the world's largest computer manufacturers.

So how does Dell market these computers? It markets to individuals *and* the community. It still uses traditional mass-media advertising to build

99

its brand image and stimulate sales; for example, DDB was responsible for the famous "Dude, you're getting a Dell" campaign, where a mischievous kid named Steven egged people on to get the Dell computer they really wanted. But they also become part of the community of customers who purchase its products. While most companies keep in touch sporadically with their customer base, Dell customers generally hear from the company two or three times a week, and when one of them needs a new computer, there Dell is.

This customer-driven business model at Dell now goes far beyond the purchasing process; for example, its IdeaStorm community, where customers post ideas and other customers rank and promote their favorite ones, currently has over 8,000 ideas and more than half a million responses. If you need technical support, its discussion forums have over one million posted messages and thousands of users online *outside* of its official channels. There is even an online studio where customers can post their own videos alongside official ones from Dell.

The concept of your customer base being central to your operations also drives the entire e-commerce industry. These sites not only nurture a community of consumers, but they also open up their storefronts to anyone who wants to be on the shelf. Moreover, they feed the dialogue between buyers and sellers by letting each of them have a voice: not only can customers post reviews and join discussion forums, but sellers themselves can also engage them with blogs, videos, product samples, and their own comments. Amazon.com, eBay, Japan's Rakuten.com and others are fundamentally changing the way we shop by putting the customer on both sides of the counter.

So, what if you don't run a major computer manufacturer or a hot e-commerce site? People who make "stuff" and sell it have been slower to bring their customer swarm backstage into their operations, particularly

The Volkswagen Polo Harlequin: a car customers demanded and got.

Reproduced with permission from Volkswagen AG.

when they have been doing things the same way for decades. How do you get from there to a participatory customer community?

It starts with having channels for customer input and using them. For example, our client Volkswagen AG once ran an advertisement on April Fool's Day in Europe for the Polo Harlequin, a car whose exterior parts were a mish-mash of different colors. It was a joke, but customers came back and told Volkswagen they actually liked it – so it went into production, and sold very well.

101

From there, it gets a little stickier if you cling to the old way of thinking. Nearly every company responds to trends in their customer input (or should). And many of us let *some* of our customers into our operations, in the form of things like market research and focus groups. But inviting the whole community in and letting them tell us what to do, every single day? That still scares most of us.

Don't be scared. I firmly believe that companies like Dell, Amazon. com, and other early adopters are trying to tell us something: Herds may listen to us, but communities demand our attention. If we do not want them to flock somewhere else, we need to build our workplace around them. If customers aren't driving your daily operations nowadays, they will soon. And those who do it successfully will dramatically leverage their brand for much greater sales and profitability in the future.

Building real communities from virtual ones

Perhaps the pinnacle of attracting a community is when people band together with each other, online or in the real world, because of their connection with your brand.

When you purchase a new Harley-Davidson motorcycle, your dealer hands you two things: the keys and a membership card for the Harley Owners Group or H.O.G. for short. With branches on four continents, this group represents more than just a web community: It has local chapters where people meet in person, as well as regional and national events where people can show off their "hogs" and meet each other.

Harley-Davidson understands that its brand represents much more than a product: It is a lifestyle. Its published "creed" talks about freedom, independence, and not knuckling under to anyone. By sponsoring a brand community that connects people in the real world, it creates a community from individuals – in this case, over a million strong – who believe in this sense of freedom and adventure, and ride Harley motorcycles as part of that lifestyle.

Other brands build communities that revolve around a swarm's common interest and not just its passion for a product. Nike, for example, brings runners together in the real world using a virtual approach. Its Nike+ shoe is equipped with sensors that transmit information to your iPod Nano, allowing you to see, hear, and analyze your running performance in real time. You can then load this data onto the Internet as part of a community where you can find other runners in your area.

This Nike+ website appears at first glance to be a traditional virtual community, with training tips, local running information, a blog, and online forums. Where it makes the leap from a virtual community to a real one is your ability to find and "challenge" other runners, and post digital information from your own runs for others to see. With sites on every continent, Nike+ has now tracked more than 41 million miles from its members.

Nike and Harley both understand that what we want in life isn't necessarily running shoes or a motorcycle: It is fellowship and intimacy. By positioning themselves as brands that bring people these things, under the common interests their products represent, they create their own network of dedicated consumers.

Of course, the highest form of customer intimacy is when it becomes real intimacy. Many people now find love and relationships on social networking sites, and destinations like Match.com and eHarmony are quickly replacing the local bar as places to meet a partner. But most social networking revolves around persistent communities who get to know each other in an ongoing relationship, just like the pub scene of centuries ago. When you help create these relationships and give them the gift of each other, they can easily become your most loyal customers.

Taking a broader view, I feel we have turned a corner in human history, one that is perhaps bringing us back to our roots. For much of the twentieth century, technology served to move us apart. It helped us replace social gatherings with television sets, meetings with telephone calls, and the community with the family cocoon. Today a new era of digital connectivity is bringing us together again. The 1960s teenager who sat in front of a television has been replaced by a modern-day teenager with 147 friends in MySpace, and increasingly these virtual bonds are finding their way into the real world.

103

but they *reported* that centrally managed brands are no more successful than decentralized ones. Moreover, almost all of them reported that they were unable to secure consistent brand compliance across their organizations: Their internal communities were already flexing their own collective intelligence muscle.

Based on our research, we see a future that has room for a consistent brand identity *and* listening to your internal community. We call it the 70/30 rule. It means that brands still spring from one great idea, hold true to their core purpose, and use this brand as their central organizing principle (the 70 percent). But it also means that there is room for listening to your own stakeholders and adapting your own organism to their intelligence (the 30 percent).

Take the example of our client McDonald's. It is one of the world's most consistent brands. Its golden arches and spokesperson Ronald McDonald are recognizable anywhere in the world. Its hamburgers have the same consistent quality everywhere. And the majority of its global customer base recognizes the same musical tagline ("ba da ba ba baa") and slogan ("I'm lovin' it") that we use in their advertising.

At the same time, McDonald's is a master at listening to the local people who put the brand to work around the world. All McDonald's restaurants are designed around quick service, and many feature PlayPlaces for children. But in Paris you may find yourself sipping a gourmet coffee in a comfortable chair, in an environment that entices you to stay after getting served quickly, like a great French café. And its menu items range from porridge for breakfast in London to seaweed-seasoned fries in Tokyo, as well as respecting local sensibilities, such as serving lamb in India or high-quality Halal beef in Muslim countries.

We also listen in our advertising for McDonald's. For example, the man shown in the picture is fast becoming an Internet celebrity in

Professor Super Saver – an Internet star for McDonald's China.

Reproduced with permission from McDonald's China.

China: Professor Super Saver. With his thick glasses and black hat, he continually demonstrates the best things you can do with six Renminbi (about one US dollar), such as cramming people into the trunk, roof, and hood of a taxi to share a ride to the airport. Naturally, his favorite way to spend six Renminbi is on the Super Saver menu at McDonald's in China, a message that led to nearly a million and a half page views on the Internet in its first week alone.

Of course, Professor Super Saver communicates with his own community of customers. He has his own blog, gives interviews discussing his personal life, and invites customers to submit their favorite ways to spend six Renminbi – giving people with the best ideas a chance to direct one of his next ads. But more important, he is a China-only spokesperson, promoting a China-only menu, an example of McDonald's listening to its own swarm around the world.

More recently, McDonald's "I'm lovin it when China wins" promotion collaborated with its customers in an even more personal way, rallying the spirit of its people in the months leading up to the 2008 Olympic games in Beijing. A special website invited consumers to submit their own videotaped cheers for the Chinese Olympic team, with five finalists invited to attend the Olympics to cheer their team on in person.

This campaign ultimately attracted more than 68 million page views from people in China – eyeballs that would be hard to attract through simple product advertising, which in turn continues to build McDonald's brand image in China. Today, China represents one of McDonald's greatest markets for global expansion, and engaging Chinese consumers as part of their brand is a key part of its strategy.

Oscar Wilde once wrote that "consistency is the last refuge of the unimaginative." Today we need to take that a step further and say that not collaborating with your internal community will lead you from brand consistency to rigidity and paralysis.

Putting collaboration into practice

Changing the top-down way many of us create and enforce our brand identities is painful. But when you decide to harness the energy of all of your communities – your customers and your internal stakeholders – the results can be liberating, as in the case of strong brands like Nike and McDonald's that continually reinvent themselves. But this collaborative environment is now becoming more than a good thing: Today's digitally connected world will soon leave you no other choice.

One of our greatest sources of motivation comes from the collective force of people uniting behind common ideas. When you build a community around your brand, you change their view of the world, your product, and themselves, creating sustainable desire in the process.

Traditionally people in my profession have tried to create this desire on the strength of our creativity and our market research. We are still very successful at this. What has changed is that our audience is now in digitally linked masses, not just small cocoons in their living rooms. In a globally linked world, motivating people will increasingly be driven by the influence you create in both virtual and real communities.

This does not mean that traditional marketing methods will go away. We should listen to our customer, but sometimes we should also listen to market intelligence and our competitors. For example, McDonald's noticed a trend in how people drink coffee: They saw more people stopping at places like Starbucks for a latte instead of coming to their restaurants for a good but less expensive cup of Joe. Given the success of their own McCafé coffee shop in the Pacific Rim and elsewhere, McDonald's is now in the process of building McCafé Beverage Centers in many of its US restaurants. These in-store centers, staffed by dedicated and specially trained team members, feature espresso-based lattes, mochas, and cappuccinos as well as frappes and smoothies, in a transformation it expects to add significantly to its bottom line.

Would the people who currently go to McDonald's have told it to start serving gourmet coffee? Maybe or maybe not. Perhaps they might have been happy continuing to simply go there for hamburgers and Happy Meals. But by looking at other consumer communities, McDonald's is expanding its own in a way that probably would have never come from a suggestion box.

At the same time, we clearly have to think beyond traditional marketing notions like brand persistence and market share, and start looking at how we engage a community in all three levels of its needs: listening to it, collaborating with it, and building intimacy within it. The virtual world is starting to do this, very well in some cases, and in my opinion, the real world must follow very soon. This also means that we will have to keep changing our marketing channels and models to attract these communities.

Ultimately, your goal in engaging the masses is to create what Seth Godin calls a "permission monopoly": a dedicated flock that remains part of your audience and your market ever after.[7] It all starts with widening our vision from the consumer level to the community level, and how we interact with people at this level. We are now reaching a point in history where creating, attracting, and nurturing these communities can become our ultimate marketing tool.

The Third Law of Engaging a Community: Creativity

Believe it or not, people were thinking about the Internet a century ago.

The difference between those days, when people envisioned a network of pneumatic tubes criss-crossing everyone's offices, and today's online world was something no one ever imagined back then: the silicon semiconductor.

Once we harnessed one small feature of the semiconductor, namely its ability to switch between two states of logic, it unleashed a flood of latent creativity. The computer, digital connectivity, the Internet, and social networks all emerged from one catalyst that changed the way we thought.

Today I feel that the realization that we behave as a community and not just as individuals has become a catalyst for a similar wave of creativity in the way we look at marketing.

Of course, creativity is our profession's stock in trade. Too often, we still look at it in the context of the pneumatic tubes of our day: the 30-second spot, the full-page print ad, the online banner. These are not going away any time soon, but today we are in the throes of a paradigm shift that is opening up an entirely different way of thinking.

This is why I do not like hearing digital communities described in terms like "marketing to social networks," or "targeting points of influence," or "viral marketing." These are all worldviews that date themselves in this first decade of the new millennium. More important, they are only reference. Radar DDB then went to work seeding the content to influential bloggers and social media sites.

The results exceeded the target ROI within less than a week of launch. And that content is now in cyberspace forever, taking advantage of the "long tail" of specific interests: Banff content is showing up in places well outside the traditional tourism world, including sports, environmental, arts, and culinary social media, and time spent with its brand continues to increase. In the process, not one person was ever interrupted by traditional advertising.

Let's take a look at some examples of human creativity changing the way we look at marketing. Some of these are from work we have done, and others come from elsewhere. All of them reflect trends that are emerging from our growing relationship with communities instead of consumers.

Building a brand identity: Volkswagen hits the streets

We spoke earlier about how Volkswagen used a humorous video blog to help reload its image in Germany as "the people's car." Now I want to dig deeper into how this same client has been building and maintaining its overall brand image, by looking at some of the recent work we have done together in the United Kingdom.

When I was younger, most automobile ads were designed to do one thing and one thing only: sell the car. Whether it was "disc brakes from the advanced thinking of Studebaker" in the 1960s or the "wide track" of the 1970s AMC Pacer, commercials for cars usually revolved around features and benefits.

Today cars are part of our identity and image, and today what a brand represents to people is at least as important – if not more so – as specific features. As one of the largest automobile manufacturers in the world, Volkswagen has always tried to position itself as a car of choice for the masses, with a brand image as an intelligent vehicle built by intelligent people.

This ties in with a point that is very close to my heart, namely the intrinsic value of a brand. When people identify with your brand, you leave a world of constantly proving you have better features and enter one built around trusted relationships. People flock toward strong brands, rather than having to be constantly "sold" on your products.

Below are some recent Volkswagen campaigns that addressed their brand identity at three separate levels. The first one does not even mention automobiles at all: its entire purpose is defining the brand of Volkswagen more clearly, particularly among young people. The second creates a brand image around a specific car, the Volkswagen Fox, but still makes no effort to "sell" car features. The third one, a campaign for its flagship Golf hatchback, finally reaches out to consumers and their desires for the car itself.

The first campaign revolves around Volkswagen's sponsorship of independent cinemas across the United Kingdom. At first, this took the form of most sponsorship: a donation of money in exchange for public credit and good corporate citizenship. Then we helped Volkswagen leverage this relationship to extend its brand.

Part of the brand image of Volkswagen is being independent thinkers – people who look at problems differently. Just like independent cinemas allow you to see films in a different environment from your normal multiplex. And so "See Film Differently" was born.

We launched this campaign with six 60-second and 20-second spots that ran before each film in theaters, each of which featured an ordinary person giving a very off-the-wall interpretation of a popular movie. Here is an example of one take on *Ghostbusters*:

> The thing about Ghostbusters is that it's not this sort of spooky comedy. It's actually a quite serious warning about the obesity crisis threatening to take over America. You know, the whole thing is about New Yorkers basically trying to get rid of these blobby bodies that are taking over their city. The film's logo is a fat man with a cross through it – no fat people. If you look on the Internet for how many slimming aids or diet regimes are called Fatbusters – Fatbusters, Ghostbusters. Is that a coincidence? Yes, it's a coincidence. But my point still stands.

Similar spots were run about other well-known films, including a young Englishman deadpanning about how *Star Wars* is really a remake of the *Wizard of Oz* ("Luke is Dorothy, C3PO is the Tin Man, Chewbacca is the Cowardly Lion, Darth Vadar is the Wicked Witch of the West, and the wizard is obviously Yoda"), as well as a woman providing a psychosexual interpretation of *Toy Story* that probably wouldn't make for polite dinner conversation but was funny nonetheless.

A fictional amateur "film critic" gives his unique interpretation of the film Ghostbusters for Volkswagen UK's "See Film Differently" campaign.

Reproduced with permission from Volkswagen UK.

Except for the tagline "See Film Differently" with the Volkswagen logo at the end, none of these spots tried to sell you a car. Their purpose was to help the swarm who attended indie films identify with a brand that thought differently, like they did.

From there, we spread the campaign throughout a larger swarm. These spots were placed on YouTube, and the line "See Film Differently" was adopted for all of Volkswagen's film tie-ins, including sponsorship of *The Bourne Ultimatum*. We created press ads, put up posters, gave out free postcards and beer coasters, and sponsored a film supplement distributed with UK newspaper *The Observer*.

Next, we started engaging people as a community. We set up a website in conjunction with another newspaper, *The Guardian*, where people could see and contribute to an interactive film map detailing the conceptual links between films. You could listen to interviews with actors and filmmakers. And we drew people in for a chance to win their own spot by entering their own theory about a film.

From what was a small and relatively ignored sponsorship, the "See Film Differently" campaign ultimately strengthened the Volkswagen brand in the eyes of its community, reinforcing its image as a brand that thinks, while educating and entertaining everyone in the process.

Now let's jump from corporate brand image to product brand image. The Volkswagen Fox is a subcompact designed for the mass market in Europe. It has many of the same attributes that we promoted about its 1950s Beetle in our "Think Small" ads: it is small, easy to park, and inexpensive to operate.

However, it is no longer the 1950s, when Volkswagen all but stood for the concept of the small economy car. Given the cost of fuel and the realities of driving in major European cities, today's Fox needs to stand out from a crowded subcompact market. In short, it needed a clear brand identity.

117

Advertisement for the new Volkswagen Fox, featuring 30-second cartoon summaries of movies such as *Rocky* with the tagline "Short but Fun."

This battle is hard to win on the basis of features alone. Obviously, the VW Fox has plenty of things to set it apart in the marketplace: It is roomy for its size, has a four-star safety rating, and you can buy one in the United Kingdom for a great price. All of these are important differentiators. But when you focus mainly on features, you risk sounding like everyone else.

This is where we start looking at the image that people have of Volkswagen in general, and the Fox in particular. People see this car as practical, friendly, comfortable, and intelligent. So our goal was to reinforce this brand image in a way that would spread this message throughout the community.

We began our work for the next-generation Fox with advertisements showing humorous cartoon synopses of classic movies such as *Rocky*, *Jaws* and *Titanic* within 30 seconds, with an image of the car itself dropping in over the tagline "Short but Fun." Although these advertisements ran for only four days, they became a cult favorite, garnering over 40,000 website visits in their first week, as well as a strong ongoing presence on viral video websites.

While our "See Film Differently" campaign created a mindshare about VW as an intelligent car company, this campaign was designed to get people to identify with the Fox as a fun, inexpensive car within the brand image of VW. And it achieved this objective, resulting in a strong sales increase and a market leadership position. People smiled at these ads, they identified with them, and then they went out and bought the car.

Now let's look at taking things a step further, from building a brand image to creating product desire by engaging swarm members. In May 2007, Volkswagen launched a campaign called "Night Driving" for its popular Golf compact. Television, print, and poster executions explored the feelings of what it's like to be out driving when the roads are empty and you feel like the only person in the world.

On visiting the website www.night-driving.com, you are taken on an endless night drive in which you are able to explore all aspects of the Golf. A film contest lets you edit your own version of the television commercial, using extra, unseen footage. Another section of the site lets you exchange your favorite drives with other visitors by plotting them onto maps. Finally, a direct mail campaign invited potential customers to book their own nighttime test drives under the tagline "Just you, the stars, and an open road."

In the first four weeks alone, the campaign inspired more than 70,000 new visitors to come to the site. They, in turn, spread the word among their communities – a number of copycat videos on YouTube appeared, and the Dylan Thomas classic, "Under Milkwood," whose lines open the

119

campaign's atmospheric video, even jumped to number one on the iTunes audio book charts.

Above all, we reached out to people to test drive the Golf and experience not just a car, but also a way of looking at life. The campaign's tagline, "When was the last time you just went for a drive?" spoke to a human passion for independence and freedom, which we captured in words as a philosophy of night driving for Volkswagen.

The Volkswagen night driving "philosophy"

Somewhere between 3 and 4 am.

Night time.

The best time to drive. The air flows fresh and cool through your open window.

All lights seem green, the road is yours.

Night driving.

It's calm, it's effortless.

It's for the joy of driving. No rush. No need to be somewhere at a certain time.

Just feeling the road, the car, the environment.

Give yourself time. Indulge. Let every moment linger.

The music floats along,

Mirroring the rhythm of the engine.

Never thumping, never overpowering.

Just softly underlining every passing tree, house and hedge,

And transforming your simple journey into a beautiful film.

Slowly tiredness sets in.

You turn, arriving before the sun,

> Leaving your Golf,
> Until another night,
> A night perfect for night driving.

A recent ad for the Golf, the "Enjoy the Everyday" spot, builds on this personal connection between owner and vehicle. This video ad sets an electronic composition to the rhythm of someone driving his Golf every day, with changing seasons, backdrops and passengers, as well as moods that range from carefree driving on a sunny day to squabbling with your spouse. As with the "Night Driving" campaign, ads like these become part of a brand identity that the Golf is an integral part of your life and family.

The point here is that creativity exists on multiple levels in interacting with your consumers. In the past, companies tried to get people's attention almost exclusively with feature-driven advertising for products. Today we focus more on creating brand identity and brand value. In the future, marketing to the swarm will mean attracting communities who flock to specific brand images and make them their own, through multiple channels at multiple levels.

This is not the end of traditional advertising, but it is clearly the beginning of a new world where we create relationships with consumers, in perhaps the same way that people build communities that define themselves on Facebook. It is a world where people put less trust in being told what to do, and more trust in this sense of community.

Now let's focus on an example of attracting a community of people for a very specific demographic group: male beer drinkers.

A graduate course in helping men enjoy "Bud Light"

A distinguished-looking professor strides across an ivy-covered campus as he starts to recount his school's accomplishments. "The saga began in

1922 with first successful tea party. Since then, the Bud Light Institute has continually found ways to keep women occupied, so men could go out with their friends and maybe have a cold, refreshing Bud Light." He then lists some of the school's other milestones, including the shoe sale, the soap opera, the telephone, and their 1971 invention of feminism (shown with the newspaper headline "Women demonstrate for rights as supportive men go fishing.") Wrapping up in front of an assembly of hundreds of white-coated scientists, he proudly proclaims, "We were there then, we're here now, and we'll be there for you tomorrow. We're the Bud Light Institute, and we love you."

What led to this beer company's tongue-in-cheek foray into academia? A very serious cultural and marketing challenge. Anheuser-Busch's Bud Light, the best selling beer in the United States since 2001, was under pressure from another light beer in Canada. In response, the Bud Light Institute became one of the most hilarious examples of the true power of a big idea.

It started with a seemingly simple insight that occasionally men need to mentally and physically escape the trappings of adulthood and just hang out with the guys. The idea that Bud Light could actually help these unfortunate men launched a cultural phenomenon in Canada – one that engaged men to spread the brand message of Bud Light themselves, by extending a creative idea into real-life channels such as products and an interactive contest.

DDB in Canada was part of a team that created the fictitious Bud Light Institute, dedicated to providing ingenious solutions to everyday chores and responsibilities so guys can get out with their buddies more often and have a beer. Whether it be a team of Vikings to break-up a dull family event, a 48-hour long movie to occupy your spouse for an entire weekend, or a line of greeting cards to help get you out of the odd jam – the Bud Light Institute is working on it.

To be truly effective the team consistently brought the Institute to life beyond traditional advertising. They held PR events, created in-bar promotions, and online interactive elements to help convince consumers that the Bud Light Institute actually exists.

A building in Downtown Toronto was wrapped with a "Coming Soon" Bud Light Institute Headquarters message. Newspaper ads announced new appointments at the Bud Light Institute, and a contest was even held to select a consumer as the Summer CEO for the fictitious Institute. Incredibly, 1200 resumes were submitted and 200 people showed up for the final interviews, and the resulting media event attracted television, radio, and print publicity.

The next year a CD was produced to help ensnared guys called "Ulterior Emotions". The CD was promoted on television and then offered online for free at the Bud Light website. Radio station promos were negotiated in major markets and the full-length songs created for the CD were given free airplay by Canadian DJs. The CD was later made available through HMV, one of Ontario's leading music retailers, and eventually reached number 14 on HMV's National Best Seller's Chart with more than 40,000 CD's ordered by consumers.

An actual line of greeting cards followed and was made available to consumers online. Sample sentiments included: "I didn't want to wake you ... So I Stayed Away All Weekend," "Let's make February 15th Our Valentine's Day," and the ever-popular "Happy Belated Anniversary."

This campaign produced more than three straight years of double-digit growth for Bud Light in Canada; it created a brand that consumers loved to spend time with, and a number of ingenious escapes to allow them the time to get together. Above all, its creative humor got men themselves to become agents for the brand, in a successful effort that more than doubled brand awareness for Bud Light and made it the fastest growing beer for its Canadian distributor Labatt's.

124

One of a series of tongue-in-cheek greeting cards for men from the Bud Light Institute.

Reproduced with permission from Anheuser-Busch.

The high-tech fashion accessory in your ear: Phonak's Audéo

Getting people interested in beer is one thing. But what about getting them interested in a hearing device?

For most people, purchasing a hearing aid sounds about as hip as breaking one's hip. For Swiss manufacturer Phonak, this represented a marketing opportunity to reach a population who want to hear better but don't think of themselves as elderly: a group that ranges all the way from children born with hearing problems to baby boomers who have been to too many rock concerts.

Phonak's website for its new Audéo device has barely a touch of grey among the dozens of people you see: a young woman standing in the rain, a couple nestled under the covers, a female billed as a former punk rocker, even a heavily tattooed beach volleyball player. You also won't find the words "hearing aid" anywhere in the copy for what is now billed as a Personal Communications Assistant (PCA).

The website's frequently asked questions section continues this theme, talking about things like whether other people will see the device, or how you can change its design scheme. It comes in bright colors, like iPods. And you get fitted for one by someone it refers to as "your Audéo specialist," as opposed to a hearing aid salesperson.

What is perhaps more significant is that this campaign quickly became picked up on the wings of the blogosphere: in particular, talking about the incongruity of using a very hip approach to sell a medical product that is often associated with old age and declining health. But in getting people's attention about the advertising, it also stimulated a dialogue about the device itself.

In the process, this campaign created a new frame of reference for hearing devices, one that is framed around human wants and needs – and particularly, in this case, targeting these messages toward a demographic that might not have thought much about using technology to improve their hearing. Here is how Phonak frames the website description of Audéo:

> Social interaction is what makes us feel alive. Communication is the basis for all our relationships, so understanding every nuance of conversation is crucial. But sooner rather than later, our active lives begin to catch up with us, as gradually our ability to distinguish higher pitched sounds diminishes. If demanding listening situations have become a challenge, it's time to make the simple decision that will keep you in control.[1]

Of course, not everyone buys into this reframing of the marketplace, as evidenced by this quote from the Adrants blog:

> On one hand, the shift towards making hearing aids cool seems misguided since they aren't . . . On the other hand, with the aging of baby boomers who (still) don't want to admit they've become responsible adults, this hippication of the device makes perfect sense. It plays directly into the notion many 50 year olds still think they're still cool enough to regularly hang out with 25-year-olds. It's all about youth, baby.[2]

Even more interesting are the comments that follow this piece, many of which were from younger people with hearing loss who appreciated Phonak trying to de-stigmatize these devices – particularly, in such cases as children with congenital hearing issues. So the community itself had an emergent opinion that did not necessarily agree with every blogger.

This, to me, is the essence of using a strong brand image to attract communities: creating a message that spreads by itself through factors that attract a specific group toward you, and stimulates dialogue among group members. These are timeless principles of brand identity in general, and loom even more important today in a digitally connected world.

Personally, I feel this is a great example of attracting a unique swarm, and even though it didn't come from my company, I tip my hat to it. So what about you? If you consider yourself a younger middle-aged person and still like to crank up rock music and have a good time, what hearing aid would you plan to look at first?

Giving a local company a global identity

Do you know where the Dutch city of Apeldoorn is? Many people outside the Netherlands do not. But some creative marketing made this midsize town in eastern part of the Netherlands famous and part of a widely known saying.

Centraal Beheer is a direct writer insurance agency in the Netherlands. It is not flashy, and it has been around for a long time. And it is based in Apeldoorn. The centerpiece of its marketing is a series of humorous videos that have long defined its brand, and now have spread virally on the Internet.

Our "Acupuncture" spot, for example, shows a Caucasian man visiting a Chinese acupuncturist in a walk-up clinic on an upper floor of a downtown building. The doctor, who does not speak the visitor's language, blithely keeps sticking him with needles until he suddenly realizes that the building is on fire – at which point he unceremoniously grabs his bag and leaps out the window, three stories down, to a waiting trampoline held by the fire department.

The hapless patient stands in the window of the clinic, watching the trampoline below, knowing that he has dozens of acupuncture needles still sticking out of him. As he ponders what to do with a scared look on his face, the tagline appears: "Just call Apeldoorn."

Other ads take a similar idea of putting people in awkward situations; for example, one spot featured someone moving to a small town anonymously as part of a witness protection program after testifying against the mob, only to be greeted with massive crowds and live news crews as the town's 100,000th resident. Another one shows a cautious van driver making a sudden stop to avoid hitting a family of geese crossing the road – and then bursting into tears as the elaborate wedding cake in the back smashes into the driver's rear window.

As always, the tagline is "Just call Apeldoorn" – followed by a simple ID of Centraal Beheer as "The insurance company in Apeldoorn." This tagline has become such a common phrase that Dutch people often use it as a generic response when something bad or stupid happens, and it even ended up in the dictionary.

"Acupuncture" was critically acclaimed in our industry, winning a coveted Cannes Lion award for DDB in Amsterdam. But even more interesting is that this and others like it spread through channels like YouTube and the blogosphere, garnering thousands of links on the web and extending its reach far beyond traditional advertising. The "Acupuncture" spot alone has now logged well over one million views online.

Above all, ads like these reinforced a longstanding brand message. What do you want when something bad happens? You want somebody to help you. The ads convey two core values for a direct writer: personal contact, because although there is no broker, there are people in Apeldoorn that will help you with all you need. And simplicity, because all it takes is a phone call. And these ads, which make people laugh and get spread far and wide through the Internet, reinforce this promise. That is why, even when you are a local agency, you can leverage social media to get everyone in the Netherlands – and quite a few people in Europe and beyond – to know where Apeldoorn is.

The link between traditional advertising and community influence

Why do we call daytime television dramas "soap operas"?

The answer, of course, is that they were historically sponsored by household cleaning products. These shows represent one of the classic examples of herd advertising, dating back to the early days of television; for example, the American show *As the World Turns* has been continually in production since 1956.

Today, more than half a century later, how we look at media like these makes an interesting case study of influencing people, and in my view form a nexus between traditional advertising and the kinds of social community marketing that we need to be doing in the future.

Among Spanish-speaking viewers in the US and Latin America, daytime soap operas are an important moment of respite, and a time to feel and express emotions. We know a typical viewer watches her favorite "telenovela" for a full hour each day during the week, often with her family. Moreover, unlike typical US "soaps," a "telenovela" will only last for six months, and its audience is devotedly loyal while it is on air.

It was within this context that we and others worked with The Clorox Company to turn its latest sponsored soap opera *Dame Chocolate* into a social marketing event. A bittersweet story of love, betrayal, and chocolate; its storyline involves a young naïve Mexican heiress who is stripped of the secret recipe to a chocolate fortune after being betrayed by her first love, an American relative living in Miami, and comes back with a vengeance.

A collaborative effort between DDB, Clorox, and concept developers FiRe Advertisement, together with production partner Telemundo/NBC, *Dame Chocolate* helped define a new relationship between branding and entertainment. It went far beyond the bounds of a traditional sponsored show, to become a unique event where Clorox products became part of both the story and the lives of its viewers.

Given the bond between the show and its audience, we knew that an effective connection with our brands had to be organic and nonintrusive. The opportunity was for the Clorox brands to become characters in the story with an emotional connection, not mere "product placement," and so we built these relationships at several levels:

- Clorox products became an integral part of the plot, in keeping with its brand theme of health and wellness. For example, Clorox laundry products are used to clean blood evidence from clothes to save an innocent person from going to jail, and storylines are created around using other products to protect a sickly baby, a hospital, and the chocolate factory.
- Clorox products are present as part of the daily lives of the characters. Maids use CLOROX® cleaners around the house, the secret ingredient for the pivotal chocolate recipe is transported from Mexico to Miami in a GLAD® food bag, and the leading man races in a KINGSFORD®-branded car similar to the one sponsored by Clorox in NASCAR.
- Show tie-ins linked products in stores to the show and its plot. For example, Clorox's POETT® floor cleaner was produced in a limited edition "Love Secrets" package that allowed consumers to experience the scent of the secret flower ingredient in the main plot.[3]
- Perhaps most important, real-life events brought the show and its sponsorship to life for people. Branded calling cards were distributed to consumers, a limited edition DVD and cast bus tour were launched, and point-of-purchase displays were created in major stores.

The result was a show that helped Clorox products build a more personal relationship with Spanish-speaking consumers. *Dame Chocolate*

130

eventually became the number one show in Puerto Rico, Panamá, Costa Rica and Ecuador, as well as a success in US Hispanic prime time, and the show was extended for 30 extra episodes.

Above all, this very creative and multifaceted campaign represents an outreach to an untapped market that wants to make a connection with these brands. Giving people something important, while sharing a brand that revolves around freshness, cleanliness, and health, takes the classic rationale for the soap opera in a fresh new direction for the twenty-first century.

CLOROX® cleaning products integrated into the plot line of the telenovela
Dame Chocolate.

©2007, Telemundo Television Studios, LLC and The Clorox Company. Reprinted with permission.

131

This kind of evolution – from advertising a product to integrating a brand with your life – is an example of where we are all heading. This, to me, is where marketing at a community level carries on the traditions of my profession as a social catalyst. Our founders often said that great advertising made poor products fail faster, because more people found out about them sooner. The higher purpose of our role is to open people up to positive realities that improve their lives in some way. Today we can simply do this faster and with more leverage than ever before.

Creativity in a world of connectivity

At the end of the day, does marketing to digital communities mean finding ways to better exploit online, viral, and social network channels to sell our products? In my view, no.

According to May 2007 figures from eMarketer, advertising on social networks is projected to increase more than eightfold by 2011, to nearly four billion dollars a year worldwide. However, much of this refers to *herd* marketing on social networks: things like putting banner ads on site pages and the like. Since two-thirds of Americans use social networks, with similar figures in other countries, it is clearly a large market that makes sense as an advertising medium.

At the same time, do not mistake a banner ad on someone's MySpace page for building a digital brand community. When someone likes what he sees and clicks on a banner, it is little different from someone who sees a good television spot and takes action, with perhaps a little more immediacy. But if you are hoping that this person will send his friends, and their friends, flocking toward your brand, you probably need to rethink your strategy.

Tomorrow's community-level marketing spreads influence by building trusted brand relationships; for example, a recent Forrester research report notes that "marketers should be prepared to engage in a personal relationship with users by providing something of value."[4] My view is that we have already entered an era where content, not salesmanship, represents the keys to this community.

Suppose, for example, you create some information that adds value to people's lives. Blogger Lee Odden talks about what he calls "the currency of social networks," mentioning that while he normally ignores traditional

PR or advertising advances, when he gets a report he really likes, such as a recent one on search engine optimization, he passes it along to his swarm: He bookmarks it on Del.icio.us, e-mails it to friends, and plugs it in his blog (and its feed).[5]

This is where the emergent nature of the digital community comes into play. Go to a social bookmarking site like Del.icio.us and see what *they* think is important. Visit Technorati.com and see what blogs people are reading. Do a search and see what rises to the top. My guess is that you will find content that benefits people in some way.

This is where the next revolution in marketing really lies, in the thought shift from pushing products to improving lives. The past generation of advertisers succeeded around who could impress you the most, but the next generation will succeed in proportion to how much they can serve you. This, in turn, will be a catalyst for some of the most creative thinking we have seen in a long time.

Take the truth® (with a small "t") campaign that was funded by the American Legacy Foundation to convince teenagers to stop smoking. This campaign was conceived by teens themselves, connecting with people in ways that adult "preaching" would never reach. Best known for its very dark and graphic ads about smoking risks and the tobacco industry, it seeded its presence through a website, interactive peer communications, placement in youth media, and even a live bus tour.

The outcome of this grassroots effort was that nearly 22 percent of all teens who stopped smoking did so following exposure to the truth® campaign, with more than 300,000 fewer youth smokers by 2002. Moreover, there has been a permanent drop in the rate of smoking among teens that continues to this day.[6]

So how much herd advertising would you need to reach a 22 percent market share? Could you even do it? Getting teens not to smoke is not exactly a high-demand, high-desire marketing mission like selling them iPods. But this campaign spread a message that got into people's faces and reached them, leading to real social change.

Perhaps the key aspect of this campaign is that it was not a marketing message from on high: It revolved around teenagers who participated and reached their own conclusions, and in doing so found themselves as part of a community.

In a similar vein DDB in Sydney recently launched a powerful new social change campaign for client NAPCAN (National Association for the Prevention of Child Abuse and Neglect), headed by a confrontational television commercial entitled "Children see, children do."

This very graphic and disturbing spot shows children mimicking the behavior of adults in their lives, starting innocently with a daughter miming her father on his cell phone, and moving quickly into smoking, road rage, and domestic abuse – finally ending with a man about to punch his cowering wife on the floor, with his young son's fist cocked in imitation. Timed to coincide with National Child Protection Week, it was designed to get people talking about how thoughtless, aggressive, self-centered, and violent behavior by adults is copied and continued by children.

134 Scene from NAPCAN Australia's disturbing "Children see, children do" video on domestic violence and abuse.

Reproduced with permission from NAPCAN Australia.

This 90-second spot, which was also supported by a print campaign and ran across broadcast and cable television as well as cinemas, emphasizes the need for adults to set a good example and break the cycle by making their influence on the next generation a positive one.

Examples like these make what I feel is the most important point about creativity and social media. We are not just in the business of selling products. We are in the business of selling ideas. Some of these ideas lead people to buy things, but increasingly they should lead people to flock to your brand. And many of these ideas should change the way we think and improve the quality of our lives.

Reaching people with these ideas is not about a specific technique. It is not even about social networks or viral videos. It is about continually finding new ways to connect with communities, increasingly by offering them things of value or content that attracts them. This means that the product-centric view of selling things is giving way to the swarm-centric view of providing information and building communities. I believe there is no profession better suited to this kind of creativity than the one I am part of.

135

8

Attracting the Swarm

Samuel Brennan knew how to get people to flock to him.

Brennan, a newspaper publisher and religious leader in the frontier California of the 1800s, noticed that some of his church members were paying tithes in precious metal – powdered gold they had discovered working at a mill. So one day he went up and down the streets of San Francisco waving bottles of this powder and yelling, "Gold! Gold from the American River!" Before long, word had spread clear across the country, and thousands soon traveled great distances to descend on the area.

Incidentally, Brennan had first purchased every shovel in town. Selling mining equipment made him the first millionaire of the California Gold Rush, and helped turn this sleepy and isolated village of 1000 people into what is now one of the world's leading cultural centers.

So what kinds of gold can you and your brand wave in front of the swarm to attract them? And what will they buy from you once they arrive?

We just looked at what I see as three competencies that are central to marketing to digital communities: conviction, collaboration, and creativity. Now, I would like to take this a step further, and look at the piece that pulls all three of these together: What is it that *attracts* these people?

When you look at how a swarm of bees behaves, there are lots of things going on: how the bees communicate to the hive, how the swarm chooses a likely food source, and how they follow each other. But ultimately, it all boils down to the nectar in the flowers. Let's take a look at what kinds of nectar will engage the People 2.0 generation and attract them to your brands in the twenty-first century.

A case study of attracting a new audience: Monopoly Here & Now

Brennan succeeded with his customers by creating a monopoly, which neither I nor the laws of most countries encourage. But one of our greatest successes in building a new customer community at DDB involved creating a very different kind of Monopoly: the new Monopoly Here & Now game.

How does this sound for a marketing challenge? Launch a board game in an era when most families are off watching television or surfing the web. And not just any board game, but a 70-year-old one that is already owned by 75 percent of families, costs a third more than the regular version, and is being released in the summer, when sales are traditionally less than 10 percent of their peak during the holiday season.

This was the situation we faced with the release of Hasbro's Monopoly Here & Now game in the United Kingdom.

Our market research bore out the task ahead of us. Many people remembered Monopoly fondly from their childhood. They also remembered that games could take hours or days. And in a world with less family time and short attention spans, many of these people had little or no interest in picking up a board game again – until we pulled out a set and actually got them playing. Then they loved it.

So for us, this new seventieth anniversary edition became an opportunity to reestablish one of Hasbro's core brands – as long as we could get them engaged in playing the game again, and if people started engaging *each other* to play it.

Monopoly is a real estate game, with its UK version based around landmarks in London. Hasbro's new Here & Now version was updated to reflect twenty-first century London, from new neighborhoods to current real estate prices. Even the game pieces were updated with artifacts of current urban life, including a cell phone and a rollerblade. This soon gave us an idea that became a classic test case for swarm marketing: Why not use the entire city of London, linked through the Internet, to play a live version of the new game?

This is the idea that led to the birth of Monopoly Live: a month-long event where tens of thousands of people played the game as it unfolded in real life. Instead of game pieces, we had specially painted cabs with GPS systems. As they made their normal rounds, the places they passed by were linked to squares on the board. Everyone who signed up to play was given 15 million GBP of "Monopoly Money" to buy properties and collect rent from wherever the cabs went. And the grand prize winner had his or her real-world mortgage paid for a year.

We used traditional advertising to launch the game, including taking over the main page of Yahoo! the day it started, but from there the word was spread by the swarm: Over 300 quality blogs mentioned us, and we garnered substantial player PR through online chat. Soon over 40,000 players made nearly a quarter-million visits to the game site. By the time this one-month campaign was over, annual sales of Monopoly for 2005 were up by 35 percent, seasonal sales for that month grew by over 200 percent, and something magical happened that continues to this day: Monopoly was suddenly very current and hip again.

Today we still market Hasbro's Monopoly game by engaging its customers. Recently, for example, the game's mustachioed flagship character Mr. Monopoly appeared throughout the media to promote a new way to engage its brand community: voting on which cities around the globe would appear on the board of the new Monopoly Here & Now

The twenty-first century London skyline graces Hasbro's 2005 UK edition of Monopoly Here & Now.

MONOPOLY © 2005 Hasbro. Used with permission.

140

World Edition, coming out in 2008. Versions in specific countries also have popular landmarks that were voted on by players. And today we are finding new ways to keep the conversation going.

Advertising is passive. Entering a contest is only slightly less passive. But playing a familiar game online against other people, with the chance to earn real money, started people flocking toward us. People soon developed their own strategies: For example, one person wrote about acquiring Wimbledon real estate just before its famous tennis tournament. Above all, they talked and competed with each other.

Ultimately this campaign wasn't just about a new game – it was about how London had changed in the twenty-first century. Building a game around recognizable places put a fresh spin on a game that many Britons grew up with, and using current real estate prices got people talking about how much had changed in one of the world's most expensive cities. So it became part of a dialogue on modern life and not just a marketing promotion for a product.

It also stood the demographics normally associated with online games on its ear, with older players spending more time than younger ones. Some people even signed in to play every day of the entire month-long contest, with the average person playing three times. And perhaps the biggest outcome was that it built a new brand community around a very old game, with over 100,000 names signed up for future marketing activities.

On a personal level, I feel the pride of any good communications person when something succeeds in a big way: We proposed a campaign that went far beyond our client's original marketing budget, and delivered results that were a factor of two beyond what we projected from it. It taught both DDB and the world a powerful lesson: Attracting a new

141

One of the real London taxicabs used in Monopoly Live in 2005.

MONOPOLY © 2005 Hasbro. Used with permission.

community to your brand has a potential that goes far beyond our traditional focus on retail channels.

Now, let's look at some of the mechanics of attracting these communities.

Targeting the influencers

Think of your favorite brand.

Now answer the following question: Would you recommend this brand to a friend or colleague?

This single question is at the heart of the Net Promoter Score (NPS), an approach that correlates corporate growth with how many customers answer that question. First developed by Fred Reichheld at Bain and Company, it is now in use at major firms like GE, Procter and Gamble, American Express, and others.

Whatever you think of NPS as a measure, it is part of a much greater trend: learning not only who will use your product or service, but also who will spread the word to others; in other words, learning who are the influencers.

For example, advertising to recruit people for the US military has traditionally been aimed at potential recruits themselves – just like nearly any advertising for anything. But in the early 2000s, the military looked critically at who influenced people to join or not join the military, and found another group: parents.

According to figures from Army-sponsored studies, parents were by far the biggest influencers in a person's decision to join the military, as well as a growing source of opposition to enlistment, particularly with an all-volunteer force engaged in two wars. So the Army launched a campaign around educating parents about the benefits of being in the military, including career paths, college assistance, and personal growth.

An image from todaysmilitary.com, a US Army recruiting site aimed at parents.

Courtesy US Office of the Secretary of Defense.

The resulting video ads challenged parents to know what to say to children who wanted to enlist, sent them to a website (todaysmilitary. com) with more stories and information, and were tied in with a broader campaign including direct mail and personal outreach.[1]

Did it work? The results are not clear, in what remains a tough recruiting environment and an ongoing national debate about US military involvement. It is hard to tease out the specific influence of campaigns like these. But it does point to a broader trend, which is to seek out and engage people who can influence a community, and not just the end consumer.

Now let's look at campaigns that are often incredibly successful in targeting people who influence the swarm: the promotional efforts behind films that are vying for the Academy Awards, best known as the Oscars, in the US movie industry. Winning an Oscar is the height of achievement for anyone in that industry.

Once upon a time, the path to an Oscar winner was to release a blockbuster film that both grossed a lot of money and pleased the public. For example, the 1997 movie *Titanic*, which was the highest grossing film of all time with nearly US$2 billion in receipts, also won the Academy Award for best picture. For many years the top Oscar awards often, but not always, followed the herd marketing dictum that bigger was better.

Now the formula has changed toward targeting influencers first. It is not unusual for a film with Oscar hopes to go into very limited release toward the end of the year, with the main target being critics – and what they will say to other critics – to create the buzz that ultimately leads to the Academy vote.[2]

This means that size often no longer matters. For example, the most recent best picture award in 2007 went to the film *No Country for Old Men*, which grossed a relatively modest US$75 million – less than a third of what *Titanic* cost to make in the first place – and was somewhat of a cult favorite whose audience grew slowly. Movies are a microcosm of how marketing is now looking beyond "How many consumers can we attract" to ask, "What influencers can we reach."

But my view is that the whole question of influence does not stop there – which leads me to my next point.

Targeting everyman

When we think of influencers in the herd marketing era, we automatically tend to think of people with the biggest soapboxes: media figures, celebrities, and professional reviewers. In the Web 2.0 era you can add influential bloggers and cyberjournalists to the list. But now, as we look at engaging digital communities, our target audience of influencers is increasingly looking like you and me.

In a world of social media, you don't necessarily even need to know who influencers are or contact them personally. For example, many bloggers monetize their sites by allowing people such as Google to serve ads on them; and now, there are firms such as BuzzLogic that will allow you to target your ads based on the content of the actual blog conversation.[3] In cases like these the community itself becomes the source of its own influence, and chooses its own advertising.

This, to me, is the heart and soul of the new digital age of influence: Instead of emanating from people at the top, influence emerges from consumers themselves. And in the process, our message target must evolve from a massive herd to these emerging influencers: the darting fish who lead the rest of the school to follow them. In much the same way that power has shifted from kings and emperors to swarms of voters, the migration of influence to linked masses of consumers will change the way we think about marketing.

We spoke earlier about how communities often flock or flee based on the influence of any one member. A flock of birds will take flight in unison if just a few of them are startled, and just one convincingly worded review on a website can send people to – or keep them away from – your hotel or restaurant.

So if anyone can influence a digital community, how do you target points of influence? The simple answer is by understanding the nature of the community itself.

Have you ever eaten at a Japanese restaurant with a koi fish pond, and watched the hungry fish practically climb out of the water over each other as you tried to feed them? You didn't specifically target the right fish. Instead you created conditions that let the nearest fish start a chain reaction that eventually got all of them flocking toward you.

The same thing is true with your brand. When you create excitement and enthusiasm among your community, influence spreads itself. Look at the release of hot products like the Wii game console or the 2005 Ford Mustang: Once the first samples were seeded to the swarm, all the other "fish" – the reviewers, the thought leaders, the bloggers, and ultimately the customers – came flocking to the product. Likewise, when your brand is trusted, the growth in your customer base is often self-sustaining as people flock to you and bring their friends along.

Just remember that influence of everyman goes both ways in an era of digital connectivity: They can lead others to quickly flee as well as flock. For example, in June 2006 an AOL user by the name of Vincent Ferrari recorded his experiences trying to cancel his account with an aggressive and uncooperative phone rep. and then posted it to his blog.[4] The resulting firestorm of publicity put Ferrari in the national media spotlight, Consumerist. com dubbed his recording "the best thing we have ever posted,"[5] and soon AOL's internal retention manual was even posted online.

Less than six weeks later, AOL shut down its retention centers and switched much of their service to a free advertiser-supported model. It remains an open question how much the Ferrari incident affected this decision, but the lesson for all of us is that any one consumer or disgruntled employee now has the power to spread their message about your brand.

At the same time, the power of "one" is clearly tied in with your existing brand identity. You can equate this to how sensitive animals are to the "noise" of individual inputs. If you have a great brand and someone complains about a single bad experience, people tend to filter it out; if you don't believe me, check Google sometime to see how the swarm treats "peer" brands versus "predator" ones. But if your brand image is one that too many people love to hate, a single voice can rally an unstoppable swarm, and aim it straight for your bottom line.

This, to me, is the nexus of herd marketing and digital communities. The heavy lifting of creating a strong brand not only isn't going away, but it also becomes more keenly important. People react to brand perception and correlate what they hear from their networks with their own experience and perception.

Finding points of attraction

For decades, advertising has revolved around finding things that attract individuals to your brand. Whether it is benefits, features, emotions, contests, or something else, most of our efforts have tacitly been aimed at you, second person singular, as an individual member of the herd. Obviously we always recognized the value of good word-of-mouth, even back in the days when most of us rode horses around town; but our end product has often been a private one-way dialogue.

Now the game is changing. In the viral marketing era, we started thinking more about what gets people to talk to other people about a brand. Today we must now look at what attracts everyone who can influence a community, from the people who forward e-mail to their friends, to the blogger, to the consumer who leaves a rating comment on a website; in other words, everyone.

So what kinds of things are shaping up as the new attractors? Here are some of the things I think we need to be looking at nowadays.

Intimacy: Why do people read blogs or hang out on social networking sites? It is not just to read someone's opinions or listen to someone's music. The one thing Web 2.0 does better than anything is connect people with each other.

In some ways, social networking is better at connecting people than real life is. In the real world there are few places where you can walk in off the street, join a crowd of strangers, and start talking with them. But look at how people who comment on blogs start responding to each other, or how networks start forming in places like Second Life. This virtual intimacy often then spills over into the real world as people get to know each other as people.

We talked earlier about moving toward brand communities; the "bait" that attracts these communities are tools to connect people. As advertisers, I feel that much of our success in attracting people will revolve around rich content where they can find each other.

Take the Monopoly Live example we mentioned earlier. People did not just play the game in silence and solitude. They were part of a virtual

147

community, with interaction between competitors and a discussion forum. It was less like advertising and more like the days when you went down to your neighborhood park and started a pickup basketball game.

I feel we are just scratching the surface of building intimacy and fellowship within a virtual community. For example, one of our divisions recently attended a client briefing that looked at ways of using your wireless phone to connect with social networks of strangers in the real world. If I told you more right now they would have to shoot me, but stay tuned: I believe that the level of connectivity we have today is nothing compared with what we will have in the future.

Novelty: Think about the last time you passed something along to other people. Why did you do it? I am guessing that most of you would say that it was funny, interesting, or unique, and you wanted to share the good feelings of the moment with others.

DDB has a long history with American brewer Anheuser-Busch, and a big part of our relationship has revolved around reinforcing its strong brand identity through online and offline video advertising. In particular, our ads for Bud Light beer often show how men will do anything to get it.

148

Taking this concept to the Web 2.0 era led to "Swear Jar," an edgy Internet-only video we released for Anheuser-Busch in 2007. In it a young woman tells a co-worker that people have to contribute to a change jar on her desk if they get caught swearing, then nonchalantly replies that the money might be used to get the office a case of Bud Light.

Soon everyone in the office, male, female, old, and young, is doing business using a stream of words that get bleeped out in the ad. Men greet each other in the halls with, "(Bleep) you, Jim!" A woman in a meeting says, "Can I borrow your (bleeping) pen?" A manager leads a motivational meeting by talking about how they are going to (bleep),

Scene from the Anheuser Busch "Swear Jar" video advertisement for Bud Light beer.

Reproduced with permission from Anheuser-Busch.

(bleep), and (bleep) the competition. Even the company receptionist gets into the act, announcing over the public address system, "Will the owner of a white station wagon please go (bleep) yourself."

What made "Swear Jar" so successful was that people flocked to it online, and talked to each other about it, because it was funny and provocative at the same time – the kind of thing that makes people want to say "check this out" to each other. And in today's online environment, where some of these people are on blogs and websites, word got around very quickly. The spot was viewed over 12 million times in just over a year, and won an Emmy among other creative awards. Best of all, it kept people flocking to Bud Light as their beer of choice.

149

Of course, the key point about attracting the swarm with novelty is that it has to be, well, novel. You can't just attract the same people next year with another bleeped-out ad. But, in general, the things that make people identify with their peers – like humor, truth in jest, or even gentle shock value – will always make good bait to attract them.

Can 'bad' advertising build a brand?

The Super Bowl is one of the most widely viewed television events in the world, drawing an audience of nearly

100 million viewers each year. It is also literally the world championship of advertising. Agencies develop their best and most creative work for airtime that sells for nearly US$3 million per 30-second spot, and many people watch the advertisements as closely as they watch the football game itself.

Numerous polls rank the best and the worst Super Bowl ads after each game, and for the past two years some of the worst-ranked ads have come from the SalesGenie.com division of database firm InfoUSA. During Super Bowl XLII in early 2008, two animated spots written by the company's own president, Vin Gupta, featured a harried Indian salesman about to lose his job and a Chinese panda whose bamboo furniture store was about to go out of business, both of whom were saved by sales leads from SalesGenie.com.

Despite ranking dead last in viewer polls, and even raising eyebrows about ethnic stereotypes (for example, the Indian salesman Ramesh notes that he has seven children), both ads were a tremendous success in generating new business – and Gupta recently declared himself as being "thrilled" to have had the worst ads in the Super Bowl. The company now spends a quarter of its US$18 million advertising budget on these ads, which attract over 25,000 people annually to what is now a US$700 million per year firm.

(*Source*: Janoff, Barry, "Salesgenie Returns to Super Bowl," *AdWeek*, Dec. 28, 2007)

Scene from the "Ramesh" ad for SalesGenie.com

Reproduced with permission from InfoUSA, Inc.

Free things: Why is it that many of us never bother to check the interest rate on our credit card statement, but will bend over to pick up a shiny new quarter on the street? The answer is that we are attracted to nice things that are free. We like getting presents on our birthday, we give things to show our love, and many cultures make the exchange of gifts a central part of their business culture.

Since the dawn of time, advertising and marketing have used free things as a means to attract customers. In the era of digital communities, it goes much further than that: Giving things away often drives the spread of information across the swarm. Think for a moment about how often you search on Google or plan a car trip on Mapquest, or translate an international website on Babelfish, or listen to an artist on iTunes. Free goodies and services have become the engines that drive our social networks.

A campaign that DDB in Canada recently created for the Canadian Tourism Commission used this attraction to free things as its primary leverage. We dropped flash memory sticks around the streets of major American cities, with no CTC branding, as though a real person had lost them. These drives contained pictures and stories of a couple's wonderful Canadian vacation, along with further information about visiting Canada. Just like people pick up a quarter, people not only grabbed these flash drives, but they read the content – and in the process, became an audience that could influence their families and friends about going to visit Canada themselves.

On a broader scale, I feel that the value of what we give people free is steadily increasing. Services like Skype let you talk to people all over the world at no charge. Google will give you free telephone directory assistance at 800-GOOG-411 in the United States, or send you a text message with the address of the nearest pizza parlor. Some search engines like ChaCha even have live guides to do research on your query at no cost.

So what do you 'buy' from any of these people who lavish free services on you? You donate your time and you see their ads. We are quickly becoming an advertiser-supported virtual community whose focus is changing from selling people things to attracting them – and these, in turn, become the communities that flock toward their brand and those of their supporters.

Pleasure: Why do so many people spend so much time on the Internet these days? Part of the reason is that there are so many sensory delights waiting there at your finger tips: music, video clips, games, recipes for fine foods, and more. If you look critically at the history of the Internet, and particularly of Web 2.0, you will see that a lot of its growth revolved around the pursuit of entertainment and enjoyment.

Look at Last.fm, an Internet radio site that combines music and social networking. It takes the music you listen to and 'scrobbles' your preferences anonymously as part of a database, which it then uses to recommend and play music for you, link you to other people who share your tastes, and even show you who will be attending concerts in your area. It currently boasts more than 15 million registered users, and was recently sold to CBS for over a quarter billion US dollars.

We could go on down the list and look at all the news sites, music sites, food sites, video sites, and more out there. Most of them share one thing in common: something that gives people pleasure, which in turn attracts them as a group.

Dangling something pleasurable in front of people – not just as bait to purchase something, but as a means of attracting them into your community – is the next great principle of engaging a community. It is one of the great principles of marketing in general, of course: How many people would have bought boxes of Cracker Jack in my generation without the free prize inside? But in an era of social media, it forms a key part of how you not only attract people, but also get them to attract others.

You: Perhaps the biggest thing that I see advertisers doing nowadays to attract a crowd is giving people a chance to stand out from it. We all like having the opportunity to share our gifts, show our individuality, or have our voices heard.

The concept is not completely new, of course. When I grew up, talent shows were popular on television, and the success of today's shows like "American Idol" and their global counterparts tells me that we will probably never tire of them.

But giving people their individuality is a gift that goes far beyond showing off talent: It speaks to sharing who we are as we connect and communicate with each other.

Take Johnson and Johnson's Clean & Clear, the number one skincare brand for teenagers in the United Kingdom. Teenage girls form a large part of its market, and are a group that spends a lot of time online chatting with friends. In 2007 Tribal DDB in London launched a campaign to help them express their real selves in cyberspace.

With its "Get Your Face Out There" campaign, Clean & Clear created a website where girls could upload their own picture, crop their face from it, and create an avatar combining it with a wide range of hairstyles and animated characters: for example, riding on a motor scooter or flapping angel wings. They could then use these personalized avatars, known as "winks," in their own live chat sessions on MSN.

This campaign drew 1.6 million downloads in the first four weeks, and over eight million branded interactions. More important, it significantly improved research metrics for girls feeling that Clean & Clear was a modern brand that understood them, and that they wanted to use. Above all, it attracted teenage girls to this brand by putting *them* in the spotlight, and letting them have fun with it.

All of these attractors share one big thing in common: They tap into basic human needs and wants. But more important, they encourage responses that affect the rest of the community. This represents a fundamental shift from a "me" generation reacting to advertising to a "we" generation, whose responses signal others to follow along.

We are also talking a lot here about advertiser-supported models for the digital infrastructure that supports our social networks. As you can probably tell, I am a big fan of this model. But I also want to raise a note of caution: We must think beyond just doing herd marketing in cyberspace, where you hope to get a certain percentage of clicks from the people who see your ad online.

I also want you to think about how you can help people flock toward your brand, not just buy your product in the present moment. We need to shift our thinking from advertising brands to making them destinations for people.

Above all, we need to remember what I feel is the higher purpose of marketing and advertising: to understand human nature and then engage and attract it. In other words, it all revolves around attracting people. Today, in an increasingly interconnected world, these words are truer than ever before.

9

The Chief Community Officer: A New Agent for Your Brand

Most organizations have someone who is in charge of the product in the field. In a fine restaurant, for example, this is the role of the chef. In my field of advertising, that person is called a chief creative officer.

Chief creatives, as we call them, are highly visible people. For all of them, the spirit of their role is defined in their title: they are ultimately responsible for our creative output, namely the way we express the creative ideas we provide for our clients' products and services.

Similarly, most companies have a chief marketing officer (CMO) who is in charge of the brand and work closely and collaboratively with agencies like ours to create and promote their brand message, hopefully improving their bottom line in the process.

Our need for the unique competencies of creative and marketing professionals will probably never go away. When we want to help people define their brand and the message behind it, there are no people I would rather have in charge than the chief creatives here at DDB. But part of the reason for this is because they get something very important: Marketing and branding are a dialogue.

As we know, we are moving away from a view of the world solely defined by herd marketing. Many chief creatives and CMOs are leading this charge, jumping with enthusiasm into interactive and non-traditional work from diverse backgrounds including copywriting, art, brand management, and online work. I feel we need to see this broader view of the world resonate from the top of an agency downward.

This is why I feel the era of digital community requires an entirely new job function: the chief community officer.

The case for a community-level executive

Like the tale of the blind men and the elephant, different people see the role of marketing differently. Some feel that it revolves around things like good advertising, media exposure, and influence. Others feel it revolves around creating word of mouth among customers. Still others feel that the higher purpose of marketing is to be the voice of an organization's customers.

Here is how I see this issue. In the swarm era, successful brands will be built on a sense of community with their customers, and someone at a very high level needs to take responsibility for this community.

In fact, it requires multiple someones at multiple levels. One level may involve responding to feedback from customers. Another level may involve decisions for creating marketing activities that engage these customers. Still others encompass things like the product development dialogue between you and your brand community, or the service dialogue.

Today these are all disjointed functions that fall under a variety of titles: marketing, public relations, R&D, and customer support. Each of these roles has its own agendas and its own pressures; for example, I am sure that many VPs of customer care have goals that revolve around quality service, but daily lives that are consumed by average hold times and costs per call. Worse, many of these functions can conflict with each other unless they are steered in the right direction at a high enough management level.

In my view, we need to rethink the "box" that we tend to put marketing in. We traditionally frame the marketing process around the endgame of selling products, to the point where "sales and marketing" is considered a unified discipline by some. Open a marketing textbook from 30 years ago, for example, and you will see a focus on the traditional "four Ps": product, price, place, and promotion.

Getting from the four Ps to the three Cs of conviction, collaboration, and creativity will take us a lot closer to the original meaning of the word *marketing*: Its Latin root *mercatus* means to trade or share; in other words, create a transaction within a community. In this world a chief community officer (CCO) ideally oversees the relationship between your brand and this community, and not just the narrow confines of the point of purchase.

This principle applies to advertising agencies as much as any business, and I am putting my own money where my mouth is – and I feel where our future lies. We have recently started hiring chief community officers for some of our major DDB offices around the world. For example, take the person I just appointed as CCO for DDB's Paris office. He not only has a great creative track record, but he is also a successful blogger, video journalist, and author. Put his name and DDB's in a search engine and you will find thousands of entries. He is about as plugged in as they come.

This is where I see our own creative leadership heading in the future. As a company culture, we never were much for simply sitting around in conference rooms concocting brand messages. We have always been tightly integrated with our clients, and now we are shifting toward a closer relationship with the digital swarm as well.

Now I would like to move from my company to yours, and paint a picture of the kind of chief community officer I think you will need to effectively influence and manage your relationship with your customers, whether you are an agency or a client. I see four key roles for this person: changing thinking at the organizational level, understanding and managing points of leverage, monitoring and responding to the community, and then going a step further and serving as a community agent. Let's look at each of these roles in detail.

Change thinking at the organizational level

The term 'chief community officer' correctly implies an advocacy to the community. A good chief community officer must serve as an evangelist who works hand-in-hand with firms and their CMOs to develop a much better understanding of the communities that will help advocate their brands.

Forward-thinking CMOs have started to see the world through the lens of community, and a chief community officer can help formalize this advocacy role. Let me walk you through how it compares with the traditional view of marketing:

- Instead of simply helping companies plan products and services based on what the marketplace is telling them, a chief community officer makes sure that customers have a voice in this process.
- Rather than simply creating advertising campaigns, a chief community officer builds a community around your brand, using multiple channels among which herd advertising is just one.
- Instead of focusing on pre-sale activities and seeing areas like service and support as tacitly "someone else's job," a chief community officer takes great interest in what customers are telling the company and each other.
- A chief community officer goes beyond disseminating an organization's brand message to make sure your organization is living this message in its interactions with its customers.
- A chief community officer's primary job is to advocate listening to the voice of the community as much as communicating to members the herd.
- Traditional marketing advocates for the consumer, while the chief community officer views the community as the new consumer.

For example, Joel Welsh, the chief community officer of entrepreneur portal StartupNation.com, describes a typical day in his life as follows: record a radio broadcast, write a blog entry, meet with an online firm that links people with common interests, invite people for a community advisory board, and attend an internal audit of a new community connections initiative.[1] And that is just one day.

When you scale up these kinds of roles to larger organizations and brands, you see a role that often does not look much like traditional marketing, and yet supports customer growth much more powerfully than the classic herd advertising and influence model. It is centered on community-building efforts that, in turn, nurture an engaged customer base that makes your brand part of its identity.

This leads us to an even more central issue: results. If you were to ask me if the ultimate goal of a chief community officer was to produce financial results, what would I say?

The first answer I would give you to this question would be "yes." The second would be that you are asking the wrong question.

I feel that every job should improve the financial posture of its organization. And there should be some reasonable way of measuring this success, to provide accountability. But I am going to tell you something equally important: Too much pressure for short-term results runs contrary to the goals of working with the swarm.

161

Currently, the lifespan of a CMO's job is often measured in months, even among some of the world's largest brands; according to search firm Spencer Stuart, the average CMO tenure is less than two years. According to research from the Harvard Business School, one of the key reasons for this is that expectations for short-term performance change are too high.[2]

We know enough about swarm behavior today to say that building an engaged brand community is key to growth and success. We also know that building this community involves steps that may not immediately equate to short-term sales: things like listening to customers, co-creating products and services with them, and creating an infrastructure that attracts a community.

Sometimes you can make a quick hit with a single marketing event; for example, the Monopoly Live promotion we mentioned in the previous chapter not only dramatically boosted sales of the game, but also literally resurrected the brand image of a board game in an Internet world. But sometimes you face a multistep process where you engage your customers, they tell you what they want and need, and only *after* you provide what they want – like creating better products or building a community – do they start flocking toward you.

Personally, I feel that a chief community officer should be held accountable for engaging the community in the short term, and for financial performance in the longer term. A different set of metrics will help people get a handle on their relationship with the community, and whether they and their organization are helping it or hurting it. From there, my belief is that the financial results of successfully engaging customers will generally speak for themselves.

This same Harvard research spells out three different kinds of CMOs: a "VP of marketing" who runs a cost center for marketing services, a "classic CMO" who keeps abreast of customer trends and serves as the voice of the customer, and a "super CMO" whose authority extends into areas such as business strategy and customer relationship management.

To me, the chief community officer has a separate role, to have responsibility for building and maintaining brand communities within an organization. So while a VP of marketing may purchase an ad campaign, a classic CMO may do customer surveys, and a super CMO might hold sway over things like service policy, a chief community officer is tightly integrated with the rest of the organization. Here are some of the roles for such a person:

- Working with R&D to enable opportunities for customer input and co-creation.
- Media and online advocacy for creating and disseminating brand messages.
- Monitoring the community and interacting with it, in both internal channels (e.g., customer service and support) and external ones (e.g., social media).
- Helping the organization examine its business processes – from sales to shipping – from the viewpoint of the swarm.
- Fostering an internal culture that is in harmony with the brand.

At DDB, we are committed to deploying CCOs across our organizational network. And I am starting to see the same kind of vision across many of our most important clients. I guess we are all learning together.

Understand and manage points of leverage

A chief community officer should be someone who understands all patterns of influence online and offline, in much the same way a media planner understands patterns of media consumption. This means knowing the touch points of your brand community, studying their wants, needs, and lifestyles, and using this data to inform your marketing efforts.

How does this differ from traditional marketing? The mind set of a traditional CMO is to look for influencers: to create "buzz" among the media, the power users, the bloggers, and the industry experts. Buzz is a great thing. But today it is no longer enough.

One of the core principles of swarm marketing is that you can find influence and leverage everywhere, and a CCO should ideally be a student

163

of how these patterns emerge and dissipate. What happens when a hot new product erupts online, or a public relations fiasco draws thousands of people to the blogosphere to comment? And how should you respond to these stimuli?

I would propose that a chief community officer needs to become a student of "new buzz," the kind of influence you cannot necessarily wine, dine, or influence with a press release. Your key points of leverage were once journalists or bloggers, but today they also lie in the community's gathering places. So now you are also looking at things like what you say in a product forum, or how you "seed" new products to consumers who will talk about them, or how you handle service recovery knowing that someone could be recording the call.

As one example of where we are heading, the Word of Mouth Marketing Association (yes, there is one) lists what they see as five basic elements for marketing from person to person[3]:

- Educating people about your products and services.
- Identifying people most likely to share their opinions.
- Providing tools that make it easier to share information.
- Studying how, where, and when opinions are being shared.
- Listening and responding to supporters, detractors, and neutrals.

Notice something interesting about this list: You could insert the word "customer" in any item. For example, who is most likely to share their opinions about your brand? If you are making a hot new computer, a widely read blog like Engadget might be an important point of influence. But if your product is, say, CLOROX® bleach, people who clean their homes may be more likely to search for product information themselves. So what customers say online is every bit as important as what a pundit might say.

Dr. Laundry
Find out more about me by
visiting my biography.

Welcome to Dr. Laundry's Weblog!

Your Questions: Bleach for Dishes

Posted on March 20th, 2008 by Dr. Laundry

Q: I work at a restaurant sometimes doing dishes. The health department says that the dishes should be washed in hot soapy water, then rinsed in hot water, then rinsed in a cold water solution with 1 tablespoon of bleach per 3 gal water. I've heard that too much bleach doesn't serve the purpose and hot water kills the effect of bleach. My employer insists that the rinse with bleach

DR. LAUNDRY®'s Weblog, the official blog of CLOROX® bleach.

©2008, The Clorox Company. Reprinted with permission.

This is why Clorox focuses strongly on educating and listening to customers directly. Their own blog, DR. LAUNDRY®'s Weblog, answers questions from consumers and keeps people abreast of new products, in much the same way its customer service team serves individuals, but in a form that keeps CLOROX® visible in the search engine results that influence its target consumers the most.[4] (Incidentally, this blogger is a real scientist who has worked with Clorox for over 30 years.)*

According to consulting firm Influencer50, less than half of influencers today are traditional ones like journalists and analysts, who represented almost 80 percent of them as recently as the 1990s.[5] This means that a CCO needs to be thinking about who can influence people at every level, from good media advocacy to thinking more like a customer. Sometimes influence happens through highly placed individuals, and sometimes it happens when CLOROX® shows up in your Internet search results. Today we need to understand everyone who can lead the swarm, and engage them.

Old buzz is not going away any time soon. If a large newspaper runs a positive story about you, or the blogosphere starts talking about you,

---

* **CLOROX® and DR. LAUNDRY®'s are registered trademarks, of The Clorox Company. Used permission.**

or Oprah Winfrey chooses your book for her book club, people will flock toward you. But when you multiply this kind of exposure by what happens when people talk to each other or engage their social networks, you start reaching beyond response rates and getting small points of leverage to lead communities to flock toward you.

Brand narratives: Putting brand positioning in the hands of consumers

An important step in engaging a community is to speak their language, particularly in articulating your brand position. Brand positioning – in other words, the development of your primary marketing objective – has traditionally been the domain of a company's senior executives. But today, we see the "story" that describes a brand becoming an increasingly collaborative process involving the brand's consumers. In a DDB Yellow Paper on this subject, John Garment describes this trend with an example from McDonald's.

"Customer-driven positioning narratives are gaining traction both in practice and in the press. Larry Light, President and CEO of Arcature LLC, calls the approach 'Brand Journalism', while Nick Wreden, author of *The Demise of Positioning*, feels a better term would be 'Brand Wikization,' inferring a collective judgment through collaborative worldwide effort."

"McDonald's global marketing policy is referred to as 'Freedom within a Framework.' This policy permits local creative development around a core global strategy, allowing ideas to evolve from anywhere in the world. Many credit this approach with their worldwide business turnaround and with the success of the 'I'm Lovin' it' campaign. To restore brand relevance across McDonald's many local audiences, positioning is approached as an exercise in 'brand journalism', creating a brand story in each market with local, consumer-driven narratives."

Today, McDonald's brand promise has successfully evolved under its global CMO Mary Dillon to a concept of "simple easy enjoyment." In the view of US CMO Neil Golden, this represents a further extension of putting brand positioning in the hands of consumers, and in a recent speech to the Promotion Marketing Association, he cited founder Ray Kroc's dictum that "The more reasons we give our customers to come to us, the more they will come." According to Golden, this new brand promise represents a plan to grow by following the lead of its own community.

Sources:

Wreden, Nick, "The Demise of Positioning," Asia Business Strategy & Street Intelligence Ezine, June 2005.

Light, Larry, Speech to ISBA/WFA Annual Conference, March 2005.

Golden, Neil, "Accountability to the Boss: The Consumer" (video), Michelle Maher ed., May 26, 2008, ScribeMedia.org, URL: http://www.scribemedia.org/2008/05/26/accountability-to-the-consumer/

Monitor and respond to the community

Just for fun, try doing what your customers do some evening: Get online and see what people are saying about the products and services they use.

Search for a product by name and see how people rate it. Put in the name of a service provider and see what people are saying on discussion boards and comments about it. You might even try entering the name of a company with the word 'sucks' after it and see what comes up in your search engine.

Then go visit some of the sites devoted to discussing consumer problems, like Consumerist.com or product discussion forums. Often you will see gruesome tales of poor service, indifferent employees, or bad products. More important, you will often see posted comments on how the rest of the swarm feels about these brands.

Now, I want you to try something else: See how companies respond to these comments. Once in a while, some of them will actually post a reply explaining their side of the story or apologizing and making things right. More often than not, you will see *no* response at all. In my view, a chief community officer should be aware of what the swarm is saying and then engage it appropriately.

Straight talk from Southwest Airlines

Southwest Airlines stands out as a rare example of keeping on top of what consumers are saying about it, and engaging the community directly in response. For example, in early 2008, blogger Grant Martin published a report in popular travel blog Gadling.com about two sisters from San Diego who claimed that they were insulted and humiliated on a Southwest flight, and were then met by the police when they landed. Martin then contacted Southwest and got a very detailed response from PR manager Paula Berg, who gave the airline's side of the story. After detailing how the women behaved from their view, Berg went on to say:

"Just consider for a moment, if someone came into your office or place of business and started yelling, cursing, and flipping your customers off . . . you'd probably do one of three things 1) ask them to stop, 2) ask them to leave, 3) or call the cops. Unfortunately, when you're at 35,000 feet, you can ask the Customer to stop, but you don't have the luxury of simply asking the Customer to leave."

"When a Customer makes it clear that they are unable or unwilling to show the most basic levels of respect for the comfort and safety of the other 135 passengers onboard, we have to do something. Our Employees have an obligation to protect our Customers, and we have an obligation to ensure a safe work environment for our Employees."

"Some may question the decision of our Crew, but ask yourself this . . . 'When was the last time you were escorted off a plane by law enforcement,' and 'how many times have you witnessed someone being escorted off a plane?' The truth is these are rare occurrences."

"Anyone that has flown on us knows that we typically have a very fun, relaxed, and enjoyable environment onboard our aircraft. But when someone threatens our Customers or our Crews, we have to draw the line."

169

Compare a response like this with the terse "no comment" or stilted corporate-speak that many companies share with the public. Together with their people-oriented culture (note that they always capitalize the words Customer, Employee, and Crew), they clearly view their relationship with blogosphere as an extension of their brand identity.

Source: Martin, Grant, "Southwest comments on the removal of unruly women from their flight," Gadling.com, Mar. 4, 2008, http://www.gadling.com/2008/03/04/southwest-comments-on-the-removal-of-unruly-women-from-their-fli/.

Not everyone shares the idea of engaging customers in cyberspace. For example, one blogger complained to retailer Target about what she felt was a sexually suggestive billboard, and received a curt reply stating that "Target does not participate with non-traditional media outlets." (Ironically, this response garnered a lot more publicity than the billboard controversy itself, with the snub eventually landing on the pages of *The New York Times*.[6])

The blogosphere itself is still divided on this point; for example, when Consumerist.com posted this story about Target, many people posted comments noting that anyone can call themselves bloggers nowadays and contact organizations for comment. Still others felt that it is becoming increasingly foolish to ignore social media in today's world. As for the blogger herself, she notes that any consumer who raises a concern should expect to get a response from an organization, and Target for its part claims that it will study the issue for the future.

Organizations are similarly divided on how to handle the many corporate "hate sites" that have cropped up from disgruntled consumers or activists. According to UK risk management firm mi2g, these have grown from one site in 1995 to over 10,000 in 2005.[7] Many firms simply ignore these sites, others quietly monitor what is happening on them and respond to disgruntled customers, and still others try to actively placate the site owners and get them to take their sites down.

You might expect me to say that responding to bad things about your brand in cyberspace is a key role for a chief community officer. You are only half right. If you do a search on Google and your company has three times as many complaints as your competitors, a CCO first needs to do some internal advocacy to fix the problems. But then I do feel that one must engage consumers so that your firm is part of a dialogue, not a faceless bureaucracy that guards its response like Fort Knox.

Can you speak your community's language?

Do you think that a flock of consumers will react positively to corporate-speak about things like being strategic, customer-centric, empowered, and the like? Especially when there is a problem?

Compare that to the refreshingly candid response from Facebook founder Mark Zuckerberg when its new Beacon feature raised a host of privacy concerns and a firestorm of criticism: "We've made a lot of mistakes building this feature, but we've made even more with how we've handled them. We simply did a bad job with this release, and I apologize for it." Or Sun CEO Jonathan Schwartz, in a frank one-word response on his blog about whether his billion-dollar acquisition of MySQL had any cost synergies: "Nope."

Politicians have understood the benefit of the vox populi for many years. During the Cold War between Russia and the United States in the 1980s, relations warmed considerably when Vladimir Posner, an articulate, engaging Russian spokesperson who spoke flawless unaccented English, started making the rounds of American media.

171

Later in 2006, US President George Bush hired popular media figure Tony Snow as his press spokesperson during his second term, as he faced the fallout from an unpopular war and low approval ratings – and at a more populist level, first lady Laura Bush served as a guest host of the morning newsmagazine The Today Show, while the President himself made a video appearance on the game show "Deal or No Deal" to support a soldier who was a contestant. In much the same way, learning to speak to your community means communicating at their level, and not just with a corporate communications press release.

Sources:

Zuckerberg, Mark, "Thoughts on Beacon," The Facebook Blog, Dec. 7, 2007, http://blog.facebook.com/blog.php?post=7584397130.

Schwartz, Jonathan, "In a Vortex," Jonathan's Blog, Jan. 19, 2008, http://blogs.sun.com/jonathan/.

Serve as a community agent

Moving from brand messages to brand communities is one of those goals that sound good to just about everyone. So how do you actually make it happen?

This is where the community in chief community officer really comes in: creating an environment where swarms of customers interact with you, and, ideally, each other. One of the key roles of a CCO is to proactively engage in community-building and community-maintaining efforts for your brand.

This is not the way senior marketing people usually think. For most people, being the "voice of the customer" means analyzing safe, sterile numbers that are far removed from actual customer contact. What I am proposing is that a CCO must learn where these customers live and move there, at least figuratively.

Here are some of the specific ways that I see CCOs helping to turn customers into communities:

- **Building and maintaining communications channels** where both your customers and your organization have a voice, from traditional contact mechanisms to social networks.

- **Creating affinity groups around brand desire**, by finding points of attraction and developing incentives to connect with your brand.
- **Facilitating interactions between community members**, from virtual gathering places like online discussion forums to real ones that get community members interacting with each other where they live and work.
- **Turning community members into community influencers**, by rewarding, motivating, and empowering those who are (or could be) closest to your brand.

Sometimes harnessing a brand or product community even has an immediate cost benefit. Take customer support as an example. Some companies, like Apple and Dell, are harnessing the energy of their own best consumers to provide peer support on top of their regular customer service, through community forums that are monitored and moderated by employees.

Product communities like these do much more than reduce the cost of service, however. They harness a level of collective knowledge that few companies alone could muster, in much the same way as resources like Wikipedia emerge from the input of its users. They provide a sense of how the community is feeling about specific products and services. Most of all, they help people who identify with your product to establish their own voice.

Chief community officers help create the environment that nurtures and rewards these voices: perks, insider privileges, gifts, and perhaps even opportunities for co-creation. They can make it possible for key people to test drive your latest car, review your new computer, or go backstage for your next show. Ideally, they turn customers into partners and evangelists, and in the process turn engagement into influence.

A good CCO should also be the guardian of your online presence. Specifically, this person needs to know the difference between being on the Internet and getting people to flock toward you.

For example, right now I can hear the same phrase being uttered in boardrooms around the country: "Let's create a blog." Of course I think blogs are great things. Some of our most senior people weigh in on them at DDB. But to me, one of the first orders of business for a good CCO is to help people understand the purpose of things like blogs in the context of your brand community.

Why do your customers get online in the first place? What are they looking for? And what would they be seeking from your brand? That is what you should be asking before you create that proverbial blog.

For example, Southwest Airlines' blog "Nuts about Southwest" often features its CEO speaking openly about decisions like whether to experiment with open seating, or discussing its frequent flyer program – stuff you might actually be interested in if you fly with them – while Google's official blog offers the only official peek inside using and customizing the world's top search engine, helping it rank among the top 20 blogs as I write this. Blogs like these attract swarms by giving customers things they want.

Others use blogs as extensions of their brand. For example, Internet hosting and domain firm GoDaddy.com is famous for its racy ads, many of which get rejected for the Super Bowl, and CEO Bob Parsons uses his opinionated blog to share the saga of these ads and provide links for people to see them online. Likewise, author Seth Godin has a top-ranked blog sharing his fresh and cutting edge insights on marketing and success. These kinds of blogs reach out to things that entertain and attract the community.

And then there is the blog that serves as a forum for what a company thinks. For example, McDonald's corporate responsibility blog,

174

"Open for Discussion," is hosted by a VP who explores issues ranging from the environment to collaborative innovation. Similarly, our blogs at DDB.com look at issues that we see as important from the standpoint of a major advertising agency. Blogs like these speak to a different kind of community, one that wants to know what kind of organization you are, and whether they want to partner with you.

Moving from the blogosphere to the real world, the role of a CCO encompasses communications with the swarm at all of its touch points: pre-sale, point of purchase, customer service, and beyond. It particularly involves being present where the people who use your brand congregate. If someone says something about you in cyberspace or people call you with concerns, or there are emergent opinions about where your brand should head in the future, are you listening? You should be.

The most important thing about having a chief community officer in your organization goes beyond a job description – it is a mind set. It means looking at the relationship between you and your brand community in much the same way you look at your own family or community, as a relationship that needs to be nurtured and maintained. Marketing is a very young profession in the context of history, and I see the emergence of a role like the CCO as an evolutionary step toward creating authentic community-level relationships that lead to self-sustaining growth.

CHAPTER

10

A Blueprint for a Consumer-Driven Society

Have you ever been to EPCOT Center?

Many of the approximately ten million people who visit EPCOT each year at Walt Disney World in Florida don't even stop to realize what its name stands for: the Experimental Prototype Community of Tomorrow. EPCOT actually began life as an idea for a real community, where over 20,000 people would live in harmony with the modern world.

Eventually, the idea for an actual community was shelved over concerns about having real people and their families living in the public eye. But note what our experimental prototype community of *today* is starting to resemble: We now live in a digitally linked community where we share more of our lives, our emotions, and our preferences than ever before.

We are becoming the kind of accessible, linked public community that EPCOT may have once been meant to be. At the same time, we are also moving closer to our roots in nature, as a mass of people with collective intelligence. That is why marketing is one of the most exciting professions to be in at this point in history: We are riding an unprecedented wave of change, and at the same time setting the stage for how I feel we will influence societies for generations to come.

I recently put together my own "top 10" list for making marketing to the digital community a reality: things that need to change in the way we all think about marketing, which in turn will change everyone's relationships with the brands they use. Things that, in my view, need to start happening right now. Here is my list:

1. Look at engaging communities as a long-term process
We advertising professionals are a linked community ourselves, and perhaps more than anyone, we tend to flock toward whatever is new and trendy. Viral marketing. Branded content. Social networking events in virtual worlds. That is part of what makes this profession fun. But we need to look past catchy new marketing techniques, and focus on attracting swarms in the long term.

Take branded content as an example. I mentioned earlier how we successfully helped reload our client Volkswagen's brand image in Germany by sponsoring a funny video blog that created a great deal of buzz among consumers. Was it a success? Incredibly so. Would I propose the same approach two years from now? Probably not.

I recently came across an article about another company that tried launching a branded content series of viral videos that drew less than 50 viewers after five days on YouTube.[1] Is this a case where we did a better job of it than that company? My ego would like to think so, but my head tells me that some things are only novel for a short time. Branded content will always have its place, but as just one of many techniques available to us.

Some points of attraction are universal. Ants will always look for food. Flocks of birds will always fly away from predators. People will always seek entertainment, fellowship, and intimacy. But exactly how they seek these things will always continue to evolve. Marketing at the community level will always, in my view, be a principle and not a formula.

2. It all starts with branding
We are now entering a world where the advertiser's craft is both more important and less important than ever. And, I do not mean this phrase as a catchy piece of Zen-speak.

It is more important because strong brands are critical in attracting a community. If you do not develop and promote a brand identity surrounding your products, your services, and your organization itself, your potential customers will fly right past you.

I grew up in a world where some people shopped at store A and others shopped at store B. Today I live in a virtual world where the majority of people flock to Amazon.com or eBay, and a bricks-and-mortar world where McDonald's has twice the revenues of its nearest competitor. Yet niche markets flourish within every market segment: Good branding that defines your niche, and helps you own that niche, will help people flock toward you as well.

It is also less important because traditional advertising is now part of a different world. There are infinite numbers of channels and multiple sources of information in the path of the digital community, and advertising is now one of many voices.

The good news is that advertising still works, even in a Web 2.0 world. For example, if we put a banner ad on a social networking site, a certain percentage of people will click on it and a certain percentage of them will buy your product. The bad news is that we can influence but not control the multiplicity of channels and voices these people will see. We never were the sole custodians of your brand identity, and today the community has as much of a say in it as we do. Which brings me to my next point.

3. Live your brand message

Customers gain power and influence when they join forces in a community. This means that even the best marketing campaign can be shot down in its tracks by a swarm of disengaged employees, poor quality, or customer-surly policies. Likewise, customers who are drawn to you can become your best campaign. In an era of social media, the customers you turn on – or off – have become as strong a force as anything we can do for you.

Have you ever shopped at a store where your own brand experience had little in common with the promises of its advertising? Yet they remained in business for years or even decades? This is what I feel will change most precipitously in the swarm era. Today giants are toppling. Digital communities know what they like and what they don't, and massive shifts in customer loyalty will define this era for years to come.

At the same time, the power of truly living your brand message will be stronger than ever. People make their most cherished brands part of their identity and part of their lifestyle. When you become one with them, they will forgive your mistakes and celebrate your successes. And when people speak out online against cherished brands, the community jumps right in to defend it. It is magical to watch.

In the Web 2.0 era and beyond, we can still help define and create your brand identity. We can get it in front of people who influence the crowd. We can reinforce it over time. But beyond that, when you are out in the trenches doing what you do, your own behavior with consumers is marketing much more powerfully than we ever can. So be good, because everyone is watching.

4.   Listen to your customer community

I have this fantasy of lining 20 senior executives up along a wall and asking them two questions. The first question would be, "Do you listen to your customers?"

I am picturing every single one of these executives dutifully nodding their heads in unison. Some of them would point to how "customer-driven" their mission statement is. Others would point to how a customer suggestion influenced one of their products. All of them would agree that they do, indeed, value the input of their customers.

Then I would ask them my second question: "How were your customers involved in the design of your latest product or service?" Specifically, I would want to know how much time people like their R&D staff, their manufacturing group, and their product marketing team spent with customers, individually and as a community. Are customers really, truly part of the creative process?

I realize that embracing co-creation with customers is still a fantasy for many people. But in my view, it is one of the central points behind effective swarm marketing. Creating a brand community can no longer be something that is bolted on after the fact by a marketing department. It is something that flows from a deeper sense of engagement between people and the brands they use.

5.   Listen to your internal community

This is one of those values that seem to be frozen in everyone's mission statement. "We value and listen to our employees." Too often, the result is a suggestion-box culture where information flows just one way.

Why is it so critical to give your team a voice? Let me word this very carefully: With no disrespect intended, sometimes your customers have no vision. At least not your vision. They know very clearly what they want in the present moment, but that does not mean that they would ever ask Apple to develop an iPod. They are agents following simple rules.

This is where your internal community comes in. Your sales team knows what is or isn't selling, and where else the swarm is looking. Your customer support team knows where you are delivering quality and where you are not. Your research and development team can tell you what the future could bring. And even the most humble frontline employee can tell you what the community is thinking at ground level.

Then there is the question of harnessing the forward thinking of your own people. If you are familiar with the advertising industry, you know what our slang term is for people who develop client campaigns: We call them "creatives." I will bet there are a lot of creatives running around in your organization as well, people who can move you and the swarm closer if you give them a voice.

Companies like Apple and Google take this idea a big step further and give their employees planned, unstructured creative time. Google, for example, has what they call "20 percent time" where people are free to use up to one-fifth of their work hours to explore things that are interesting to them. At an individual level, these policies get people thinking, but at a community level they have led to the emergence of things like Google AdSense.

Whatever form it takes, engaging your internal community has to become ingrained in your culture, or human nature will lead people to look no further than their next deadline. But when you truly make this kind of engagement part of who you are, you will take advantage of the very strong force of nature that already exists between them and your community of customers.

6.   Listen to your creative community

Everyone knows that good marketing today should ideally serve as a link between your customers, your products, and your operations. Good marketing *tomorrow* should take this a step further. You should engage your creative swarm – your marketing resources and your community officers – long before your products and services see the light of day.

In the book *The Wisdom of Crowds*, author James Surowiecki makes a very convincing argument that the collective intelligence of a community far exceeds that of any individual. It also exceeds that of the people in your organization. So when you come to us with an existing product or service and say, "Market this," you are already several steps too late.

When you move the process of marketing and branding upstream, you are creating both your brand and products in collaboration with your customers. For example, traditional market research might use a survey or a focus group to see what consumers want. By comparison, marketing research in a digital community can look for patterns in terms of how people flock. So your new hotel brand can build on millions of points of existing data from the demographic group you are targeting, your next food product can build around the lifestyle and taste preferences that are built into your customers' footprints, and your next virtual community can be co-created around the community itself.

What I really am proposing is taking the age-old wisdom of putting marketing and branding first, and taking it to the next level: I want you to leverage your relationship with customers to inform who you are, what you do, and how you present your brand. Then instead of helping you sell, we can position your organization to help people buy as a group.

New Coke: Disenfranchising a community

Coca-Cola's introduction of New Coke in 1985 is often cited as one of the great marketing flops of the twentieth century. But if you look critically at what factors led up to its product launch, it represented some of the best work that the marketing industry had to offer. It just came too soon before we learned how to influence a community.

First of all, the reformulation of Coke had its birth in a very real marketing problem. Coca-Cola's market share had steadily been eroding over several decades, it had recently lost its market leadership position in grocery stores, and archrival Pepsi was touting its superior blind taste test results from its "Pepsi Challenge."

183

Against this backdrop, Coca-Cola did what any good product marketing team would have done back then. They did taste tests, focus groups, and market research. All of it showed that people liked New Coke better. Then they launched the product with a strong campaign. By any measures we normally would use, it was a great success, with an 8 percent increase in sales the next year and very positive consumer survey results.

So what went wrong? Simple mathematics. When you make a major change in a product that people have used for generations, a certain percentage won't like it – and if they feel strongly enough, will spread their influence. This small percentage started a very effective pre-Internet era viral marketing campaign, including media advocacy, an organization of old Coke drinkers, and even a class-action lawsuit. New Coke soon became the butt of jokes for late-night talk show hosts and columnists nationwide, and its mindshare quickly changed.

The lesson for us today, in an era of social networking, is to look at community impact and not just product testing. Within just three months, Coca-Cola re-introduced its original formula in the wake of a public relations nightmare. And 20 years before most people were on the Internet, we learned a lesson about consumer communities and your brand.

Source: Wikipedia contributors, "New Coke," http://en.wikipedia.org/wiki/New_coke.

7.   Make a 'numbers' case for social marketing

Not long ago, a major research organization brought together a prestigious panel of bloggers to discuss their thoughts on influencing the digital community. One of the key questions they asked was how best to measure this influence. The overwhelming answer from the bloggers was that they did not know yet.

What we do know is that simplistic approaches are not going to work. Suppose you measure how many times a piece of information is referenced in cyberspace. As soon as search engines started doing this, many virtual communities became flooded with spammers. We have adapted to this, but it reminds us to be careful that the measure itself does not change the community.

We are working on tools here at DDB that will measure the degree to which a brand message is successfully influencing people at a community level – in other words, how successfully it spreads through a community, as opposed to what percentage of individuals it reaches in a herd. Its long-term goal is to understand the mechanics of influence at a quantitative level, just like we now understand things like market penetration and consumer response.

This issue brings up a deeper and more important point. Once you can measure something, it ceases to be an abstraction and starts to become a competitive advantage. Japan learned this lesson from W. Edwards Deming when statistical process control techniques transformed quality from an abstraction into a science. Similarly, performance metrics have now ushered in the greatest era of productivity in history.

Earlier in my career at Interbrand, we devoted a lot of our energies to the question of brand valuation, and the methodology behind it. Eventually we collaborated with *BusinessWeek* magazine to produce an annual ranking of the world's most valuable brands. Today the concept of brand value has changed from an ethereal feel-good concept into something that goes on corporate balance sheets, and drives market leadership.

The same kind of transformation is going to happen once we have tools and metrics for community influence. It is when we can measure and quantify our relationship with the community – and correlate this influence with the success of our brands – that the next generation of marketing will become real for many people, and in turn drive the performance of our clients.

8. Keep learning from nature

As technological as my profession has become, it is truly ironic that the most valuable lessons we are now learning in marketing haven't come from advertising campaigns, viral videos, or CPMs. They have come from the behavior of ant colonies and crowds of people. And frankly, I have a feeling that nature has much more to teach us in the future.

In particular, one area that remains intriguing to researchers is the question of leadership and influence. Human leadership has been studied extensively, and much research has been done on leadership in animal hierarchies as well. But when it comes to things like crowds and swarm behavior, we do not really know yet if swarm influencers are fundamentally different from other swarm members.

If we could quantify and identify influencers in nature, it would naturally make my job a lot easier. While the jury is still out on this, my own personal sense is that everyone is a potential leader; for example, I share the view of some biologists that a school of fish does not flee because of the actions of pre-ordained "super fish," but rather because a few ordinary fish happened to be closer to the predator and swam away quickly. But who knows what we may discover as we keep looking further?

9. Look beyond buying and selling

One of the more interesting projects I have worked on in my career is to have served on a committee to the US State Department to enhance our image abroad.

Take a look, for example, at the image of the US in the Islamic world. Unfortunately, we often perceive their values through the lens of things like Islamic fundamentalism, while they often perceive our values as revolving around things like power and money. None of these perceived values connects with the other values.

Situations like these are more than just a PR issue. We cannot fix the image that some people have of the US as a predator by just creating a press release or making a media buy. It will take dialogue and understanding, and I remain optimistic that as we become more of a global village, our social networks will help us accomplish more of this.

This raises the broader issue that marketing is not just about selling products to people. It is about understanding how we engage and influence each other in all areas of life. People say that we are all salespeople, and the reality is that we are all ambassadors as well.

There is no question that helping people sell products is one of the things that motivates me. But one of the more exciting possibilities I see in the future of marketing is the role, I firmly believe, it will have in making the world a better place.

10. Embrace change – and the rate of change

At DDB, I often find myself quoting a saying from retired Army Chief of Staff Eric Shinseki: "You may not like change, but you are going to like irrelevance even less." There is a constant tension in most fields between change and irrelevancy, and I like being part of a field that embraces change.

I like to look at where we are going from a historical perspective, because the timeline of what we do in advertising is tiny relative to the history of humankind. Many of the cornerstones of what we do, including mass media, psychology, and quantitative measurement, have largely evolved over the past century. Popular use of the Internet is barely a

187

decade old. And social networks and interactive digital media are squarely a product of this millennium.

When we look at the field of marketing, we are holding all of this up against behavior that has evolved over thousands of years, and yet it is being brought to fruition by technologies that are still emerging as I write these words. It serves as an example of where we must go from here: riding a wave of change, and at the same time looking deeper into our own roots.

When I began my advertising career more than 25 years ago, the world was a very different place from that of my parents. Today as head of DDB, I have seen more change in the last five years than in the twenty preceding it. So the last and biggest item on my to-do list is not just to market to communities, but to evolve along with them.

***

If I could sum up all of the items on this list, they represent a fundamental change in the balance of power, away from us and our clients and toward the consumer. In an era of digital community, we are moving from monologue to dialogue to conversation.

This is all easier said than done, because we are used to controlling our brand messages. Now we have to cede much of this control to the community. On the web, no one is being led, but everyone is moving. You cannot just say, "Do this" anymore, but you can influence peers. In the future, our success will hinge less on just getting people's attention, and more on a collaborative process of inspiring people with great creative work.

Up to this point in time, we have lived in an era of interruptive advertising. We still try to get people's attention in a world where the din of voices and channels continues to get louder and more complex. Now, we are learning that the process of influencing the community turns this logic completely on its head. Engage and attract people, and no one has to be interrupted at all. Instead, they become your advocates.

An action plan for the future

As I was settling in for the long flight home from one of our offices in India recently, something struck me as I looked out the airplane window. At street level, Mumbai is a deliciously chaotic and disordered city teeming with people. But from the air, it reveals a grace and structure that is only visible as you start to see it as a whole.

That is how I have come to see brands and their consumers nowadays. My industry has often had a street-level view of this relationship, revolving around things like market research, metrics, and response rates. Now we are discovering the view from the airplane window, where we see people and their opinions coalesce to form critical forces that massively influence the marketplace.

So what will the future look like for marketing from here? Part of the answer is that we do not completely know, because behavior emerges from the individual actions of its members. So we cannot say with certainty that ten years from now that advertising on blogs, creating branded content, or opening up an office in Second Life will be the ways that we attract this community. Like the Mumbai skyline, the answers to questions like these will emerge from the view outside the airplane window as we take flight.

At the same time, some parts of this future are very clear to me. We will be engaged in conversations with consumers who have many inputs to choose from. We will attract them by offering them things they want and need. We will build our brands by learning from what they have to tell us. And we will ultimately grow our markets by helping them talk to each other as well as interact with us.

189

You could sum this all up by saying that the role of marketing is changing from creating communications to creating *communities*. Our job is to continually reach out to our brand's most passionate advocates in these communities, who spread the word from peer to peer and multiply their efforts exponentially. Our reward will be motivating these communities, drawing them toward us, co-creating a future with them, and creating sustainable desire.

In closing, I do not think everything will change. We will still need to address the herd. We will still need to create awareness, build brand images, and connect emotionally with individuals through media channels. But more and more, we will work closely with highly engaged, active brand communities. And in the process, we are entering what I feel is the most exciting period in marketing history: a future we will co-create together with the people we serve.

Notes

1 The Power of One and the Power of Many

1. "How Consumer Conversations Will Transform Business," Pricewaterhouse Coopers white paper series, Jan. 2008.
2. Kemp, Mary Beth and Peter Kim, "The Connected Agency," Forrester Research report, Feb. 8, 2008.

2 The Anatomy of a Digital Community

1. Zimmer, Carl, "From Ants to People, an Instinct to Swarm," *New York Times*, Nov. 13, 2007.
2. Wansink, Brian, *Mindless Eating: Why We Eat More Than We Think*, New York: Bantam, 2007.
3. Penn, Mark and E. Kinney Zalesne, *Microtrends: The Small Forces Behind Tomorrow's Big Changes*, New York: Twelve, 2007.
4. Wesch, Michael, Digital Ethnography website, Kansas State University, http://mediatedcultures.net/ksudigg/?p=119, accessed on *Mar. 22, 2008*.

3 Welcome to the Age of Reference, Not Deference

1. The Chinese word *Yinsi*, which translates to "privacy," is generally used in a context of hiding shameful secrets.
2. New Marketing Economy, "The New Media Mix," Oct. 10, 2007, http://www.newmarketingeconomy.com/2007/10/, accessed on Mar. 22, 2008.
3. Waxman, Sharon, "After Hype Online, 'Snakes on a Plane' Is Letdown at Box Office," *The New York Times*, Aug. 21, 2006.

4 Why Speed Is the New Big

1. Freedman, Terry, "Social Networking from a Teen's Perspective," Techlearning Blog, Nov. 13, 2007; http://www.techlearning.com/blog/2007/11/social_networking_from_a_teens.php/, accessed on Mar. 22, 2008.
2. "Now, show your mom-in-law some appreciation!" agencyfaqs! News Bureau, Oct. 30, 2007; URL: http://digital.agencyfaqs.com/perl/digital/news/index.html?sid=19531, accessed on Mar. 22, 2008.
3. McHugh, Josh, "Vox Unpopuli," *Forbes*, Oct. 7, 2002.
4. "Media Myths and Realities: A Public of One," Perspectives: Ketchum's online magazine, Issue 1, 2008, accessed on Mar. 22, 2008.
5. Rosenbloom, Stephanie, "On Facebook, Scholars Link Up With Data," *The New York Times*, Dec. 17, 2007.

5 The First Law of Engaging a Community: Conviction

1. Interbrand, "All Brands are Not Created Equal: Best Global Brands 2007"; http://www.ourfishbowl.com/images/surveys/Interbrand_BGB_2007.pdf./, accessed on Mar. 22, 2008.
2. Harley-Davidson, Inc., "Live by it™ – The Creed Film." http://www.harley-davidson.com/wcm/Content/Pages/Riders/Creed_Video.jsp, accessed Sept. 14, 2008.
3. Cruz, Philip, "U.S. Top Selling Computer Hardware for January 2007," Bloomberg.com, http://www.bloomberg.com/apps/news?pid=conewsstory&refer=conews&tkr=AAPL:US&sid=ap0bqJw2Vpwl/, accessed on Mar. 22, 2008.
4. Figures from Quantcast.com, 2/4/2008.
5. Walker, Rob, "Just Say No," *Fast Company* magazine, Dec. 2007.
6. This section is adapted from the October 2005 Interbrand white paper, "Going Global," by Jeff Swystun.

6 The Second Law of Engaging a Community: Collaboration

1. Prahalad, C. K. and Ramaswamy, V., *The Future of Competition*, Boston, MA: Harvard Business School Press, 2004.

2. Atler, Alexandra, "Reading the Mind of the Body Politic," *The Wall Street Journal*, Dec. 14, 2007.

3. Vijayan, Jaikumar, "Did Blockbuster, Facebook Break Privacy Law With Beacon?" PC World, Dec. 13, 2007.

4. http://creator.lego.com, accessed on Mar. 22, 2008.

5. Michel Gondry (producer), "Fell in Love with a Girl" (video), The White Stripes, Apr. 2002.

6. Foley, Stephen and Susie Mesure, "Mighty Wal-Mart Admits Defeat in Germany," *The Independent* (UK), July 29, 2006.

7. Godin, Seth, "Monopolies, seven years later," Seth Godin's Blog, Dec. 7, 2007; http://sethgodin.typepad.com/seths_blog/2007/12/monopolies-seve. html, accessed on Mar. 22, 2008.

7 The Third Law of Engaging a Community: Creativity

1. Phonak AG, "To communicate is to live," http://www.us.audeoworld.com/ccus/audeo_in_detail.htm, accessed on Sept. 14, 2008.

2. Hall, Steve, "Newsflash! Hearing Aids Are Cool!" Adrants Blog, June 10, 2006, http://www.adrants.com/2007/06/newsflash-hearing-aids-are-cool. php/, accessed on Mar. 22, 2008.

3. CLOROX®, KINGSFORD®, and POETT® are registered trademarks of The Clorox Company. Used with permission.

4. Li, Charlene, "Marketing on Social Networking Sites," Forrester Research, July 5, 2007. http://www.forrester.com/Research/Document/Excerpt/0,7211,41662,00.html /, accessed on Mar. 22, 2008.

5. Odden, Lee, "The Currency of Social Networks," Online Marketing Blog, Nov. 26, 2007, http://www.toprankblog.com/2007/11/currency-social-networks//, accessed on Mar. 22, 2008.

6. "American Legacy Foundation – truth campaign," Social Marketing Wiki, accessed on April 1, 2008, http://socialmarketing.wetpaint.com/page/American+Legacy+Foundation+-+truth+campaign, accessed on Mar. 22, 2008.

193

8 Attracting the Swarm

1. Jervis, Rick, "Army, Marine Recruiters Shift Focus to Wary Parents," *USA Today*, Apr. 4, 2005.

2. Breznican, Anthony, "Box office: Modest Films, Niche Marketing Change Landscape," *USA Today*, Feb. 21, 2008.

3. Leggatt, Helen, "Advertisers Target Online Influencers, Conversations," BizReport: Social Marketing, Nov. 6, 2007, http://www.bizreport.com/2007/11/advertisers_target_online_influencers_conversations.html. /, accessed on Mar. 22, 2008.

4. Ferrari, Vincent, "Cancelling AOL," Insignificant Thoughts (blog), June 13, 2006, http://www.insignificantthoughts.com/2006/06/13/cancelling-aol/./, accessed on Mar. 22, 2008.

5. Consumerist.com, "The Best Thing We Have Ever Posted: Reader Tries to Cancel AOL," June 13, 2006, http://consumerist.com/consumer/aol/the-best-thing-we-have-ever-posted-reader-tries-to-cancel-aol-180392.php, accessed on Mar. 22, 2008.

6. "Change is Brewing," Brew Blog, http://www.brewblog.com/brew/2007/12/change-is-bre-1.html, Dec. 20, 2007. /, accessed on Mar. 22, 2008.

9 The Chief Community Officer: A New Agent for Your Brand

1. Welsh, Joel, "A Day in the Life of Startupnation's Chief Community Officer," StartupNation Blog, Feb. 10, 2006, http://www.startupnation.com/blog/entry.asp?ENTRY_ID=206/, accessed on Mar. 22, 2008.

2. McGovern, Gail and John A. Quelch, "The Fall and Rise of the CMO," *Strategy+Business* magazine, Harvard Business School, Winter 2004, http://www.strategy-business.com/press/16635507/04406/, accessed on Mar. 22, 2008.

3. Word of Mouth Marketing Association, "Word of Mouth 101," http://www.womma.org/wom101/, accessed on Mar. 22, 2008.

4. Clorox Company, Dr. Laundry's Weblog, www.drlaundryblog.com/, accessed on Mar. 22, 2008.

5. Influencer50, "Research Services – Identifying the Influencers," http://www.influencer50.com/us/research.htm/, accessed on Mar. 22, 2008.

6. Barbaro, Michael, "Target Tells a Blogger to Go Away," *The New York Times*, Jan. 28, 2008.

7. Pedersen, Wes, "What We Learned Last Year: Five Issues We Must Confront This Year," *Impact*, Public Affairs Council, Jan. 2005.

10 A Blueprint for a Consumer-Driven Society

1. "If You (Just) Post It, They Will (Not) Come," The daily (ad) biz (blog), Feb. 21, 2008, http://dailybiz.wordpress.com/2008/02/21/if-you-just-post-it-they-will-not-come/, accessed on Mar. 22, 2008.

Index

203